Simple Talks
for Special Days

Simple Talks
for Special Days

Marion Prather Hays

WORD BOOKS
PUBLISHER
WACO, TEXAS

SIMPLE TALKS FOR SPECIAL DAYS

Copyright © 1980 by Word, Incorporated, Waco, Texas 76703.
ISBN 0-8499-2872-9
Library of Congress catalog card number: 79-63950
Printed in the United States of America

Unless otherwise indicated, Scripture quotations are from the King James Version of the Bible. Scripture quotations marked RSV are from the Revised Standard Version of the Bible, copyright 1946, 1952, © 1971, 1973 by the Division of Christian Education of the National Council of the Churches of Christ in the U.S.A., and used by permission.

The quotation in chapter 9 from the fable "Oliver and the Other Ostriches" is used by permission of Mrs. James Thurber. Copyright © 1956 James Thurber. From *Further Fables of Our Time*, published by Simon & Schuster.

The excerpt on pp. 114–115 is from *Anne Frank: The Diary of a Young Girl.* Copyright 1952 by Otto H. Frank. Reprinted by permission of Doubleday & Company, Inc.

To the dear girls of Burrall Class who have been at once the inspiration and the necessity for this effort.

Contents

Introduction

"Let's collaborate on a book," suggested my husband. "Just a small book. About a hundred pages. Short informal essays based on our personal experiences."

Being a woman, and especially a wife, not unnaturally I objected.

"Oh, I don't think I have enough of the experiences you have in mind. You have had them in your congressional and public life, and now in your speaking trips, in your contacts all over the world, but—"

"Why," he interrupted, "you've got anecdotes and illustrations squirreled away in that file case on the third floor that you've used in Sunday School lessons—hoards of 'em."

"But most of those illustrations are other people's experiences. Not mine," I said, as I continued to object. (I don't give up easily.)

Then he triumphantly produced an argument based on natural science, or physics, or something, which he knew I couldn't dispute because I know nothing about it.

He said, "But you are like a mirror which produces heat because it reflects the sun's rays. The rays that bounce off the mirror when the mirror is focused right generate more heat than the direct rays of the sun. . . ." He went on lecturing me, but I stopped listening. I was thinking.

Maybe the experiences I had shared with him or with others, and the years I had devoted to an effort to make the Sunday School lessons fresh and a little different, would be of use to young teachers. He could write his own book!

And so I have adapted a few of the lessons presented during thirty-three years to Burrall Sunday School Class. I have called them "simple talks" because they are unpretentious, and they are not meant to displace the works of real scholars. I hope they will be helpful.

MARION HAYS

1

Star Power
(New Year's Day)

At the beginning of each new year, it is traditional to take stock. Women may look themselves over and decide to make a few changes—take off a pound here and there, try a new hair color, buy a wig.

It's also a good time to take a good look at our spiritual health and condition and to consider whether we have changed any for the better in the past year. Or in the past ten. I once read this prayer in a devotional booklet, "Lord, help me not to primp before Thee, but to be honest about myself." To be honest about oneself, I've found, is a very painful exercise. But if we never experience any twinges, we can be pretty sure we are not being honest.

Is your spiritual diet perfect? Or does it need something extra? Jesus used the simplest and most effective of all figures of speech to show that nourishment for the spirit is as essential as food for the body—the Living Water and the Bread of Life. A child can understand it.

Jesus did not ignore or deny the needs of the body. Shortly

before the great discourse on the Bread of Life, he had fed 5,000 hungry people on a hillside just above the Sea of Galilee. The disciples hadn't been concerned about the people's hunger. They thought the people should just go home to lunch, or to the nearest town to buy some food. They shouldn't have been so stupid as to come all this distance, just to listen to Jesus, without bringing a lunch. If they didn't, that was their funeral.

But Jesus was concerned. And the heavenly Father, he told them, was, too. "He knows you have need of these things." But the soul also needs nourishment—the Bread of Life and the Living Water—which he could give them. For this purpose he was sent.

There is no basic theme that we consider more often than the need to grow as Christians. But growth at our age carries connotations which are not entirely felicitous. Some, like me, have given up the hope of growing another inch or two in the right direction and are just hoping we won't go on growing in the wrong one. But while we may be content or resigned, as the case may be, to remain static physically, that low aim would defeat us spiritually. We cannot rest on our laurels and bask in admiration of the beautiful characters we may feel we have already become. The simple truth is if we don't go forward we slip back.

What we want to be, then, are better and truer—if not larger—representatives of our faith, Christians of *star quality*.

Americans of all ages and both sexes are very fond of the imagery suggested by the stars. What greater accolade could Hollywood bestow on its highly paid actors than the designation "stars"? Our popular songs have drawn heavily on the inspiration of the night sky. (I wonder how many people who have sung, or heard, "Catch a Falling Star and Put It in Your Pocket" have remembered that John Donne used it first some three centuries ago when he began a poem with the line, "Go, and catch a falling star.") Our Sunday School songs, too, have not overlooked these heavenly bodies. One of the first of these to arouse any spiritual ambition in me was the one which put the question squarely, though more poetically, "Are you willing to be caught in heaven in a star-less crown?" Though I may have outgrown the literal concept, the ambition remains to have some stars in my crown!

Then let us aim as high as the stars. We instinctively look up when we need help, never down to our feet. The psalmist spoke for all mankind when he wrote, "I will lift up mine eyes unto the hills. . . . My help cometh from the Lord, which made heaven and earth" (Ps. 121:1,2).

When my husband, Brooks, was on the Foreign Affairs Committee of the United States Congress, General George Marshall came before the committee to make a report. He told of this incident: After the World War II Battle of Salerno, he received a letter from an old teacher of his at Virginia Military Institute asking him why he had followed the strategy he used. (General Marshall had been in charge of the military operations.)

The professor wrote, "You remember our class discussions. Napoleon, in that situation, would have proceeded like this—" and he outlined the plan of attack. "Robert E. Lee would have followed this course—. You took neither of those courses. I'm interested in your reasons for doing what you did."

General Marshall wrote back, "Neither Napoleon nor Lee had air power."

That was what made all the difference. The old strategies, even of two of the world's greatest tacticians, were worthless. The French had made a fatal blunder by pinning their hopes and their strategy on the Maginot line, an earthly bulwark, when warfare was moving to the skies.

Let's translate this allusion into spiritual terms and think of star power as the power that comes from on high.

Now, having established an aim high enough to exceed our grasp, let's come down to earth and be practical for a bit.

We had a Preaching Mission in Little Rock, a good many years ago, for which Brooks served as general chairman. Some very distinguished theologians came to take part, including Dr. Adolph Kellar of Zurich. He asked for a stenographer, and Brooks got one for him. Later in the day, when Brooks went into the office, he found Dr. Kellar chuckling over his manuscript, which the young girl had finished.

"What's the joke, Dr. Kellar?" Brooks asked.

"I dictated to the young lady, 'Salvation is a cosmic process,' and she has written it, 'Salvation is a cosmetic process.' "

The two men laughed about this very feminine mistake; then Brooks said, "Well, from her point of view, Doctor, she was probably right."

Dr. Kellar nodded. "Ya, I think she improved the line!"

Dr. Kellar had meant to make the profound statement that salvation—or religion—is a thing that concerns the universe; one of world magnitude and import. But the other side of the picture is equally true—it is an intensely personal matter! As personal and intimate as our own cosmetic process, and as practical, for it must be anchored to life. First comes the personal, or cosmetic, process. Then—and it must follow as the night the day—the cosmic. It must be born in the individual heart and then reach out to all the world.

Let's take an unflinching look at the spiritual features we have fostered over the years. Have we any warts or wens?

I think one of the most unlovely types of womanhood is the kind that gets offended easily and has a long memory for slights, whether real or fancied. I read in a family magazine a letter from a woman who must have gotten some kind of inverted satisfaction from revealing to all and sundry her complaints against her brother and sister-in-law. It was quite a list, a list of pinpricks which she had magnified. One of her complaints was of an incident which took place when her brother and sister-in-law had gone away on a vacation trip on her birthday without even wishing her a happy day! It was evident the writer had kept some little slights, probably unintentional, in her mind until they festered.

One of the insidious effects of harboring resentments is that they inevitably grow. They don't stay small and manageable; they get out of control. I used to know a young assistant minister in a church in Little Rock who served as a marriage counselor. A woman went to see him one day, not for advice or help— that is, not in the usual way. Her mind was already made up. She wanted, and intended, to pay back her husband, his brothers, his sisters and his parents for all they had done to her, and make it ten times as bad if she could! Clovis Chappell, a distinguished Methodist preacher and former pastor of Mt. Vernon Place Methodist Church in Washington, D.C., used to say, "I never met a happy hater." How miserable that woman must have been with all that hatred in her.

Most of us have some cherished prejudice we have grappled to our souls with hoops of steel, in spite of all biblical teachings. My father-in-law loved to tell about a country preacher he once knew, or knew of, who was ignorant and uneducated, but fluent and uninhibited. His frequent whipping boys and scapegoats were the "'istocrats." His backwoods audiences loved to hear him take off against them.

"And when the Great Conflagration comes, I'm askin' you," he would demand at the top of a singularly carrying voice, "where will the 'istocrats be then?"

The implication was plain: They would be out of luck—probably caught in the holocaust, like the inhabitants of Sodom.

Who were the "'istocrats"? He never said. He didn't know, didn't even know how to pronounce the word. And so his hearers could apply it to anyone they didn't like. Maybe the Catholics, or the Jews. Maybe the Republicans. Most likely the rich, whatever their religious or political persuasion. But certainly anyone— or group—that appealed to the prejudice of his hearers.

The spirit of that old haranguer is still among us, and very much at home, setting group against group, using terms that are never defined, leaving the hearers to apply them at will according to their own peculiar dislikes.

What about tensions and frustrations? Those two words cover
a multitude of situations, and every person who ever lived has
known them through personal experience. Are we stuck with
them? Must we accept irritability, depression, cynicism as inevita-
ble consequences?

Two women sitting behind me on a bus in Washington were
chatting away. I paid no attention till I heard one say, "If you
have a fear of something, you have a fear! That's the way it
is—there's nothing you can do about it."

I can almost hear the Apostle Paul say, "That's nonsense.
You can 'learn to do well' (Isa. 1:17). I learned to be content,
no matter what. I learned to lay aside my fears, and all the
weights which beset me. I learned to run with patience the
race of life." We are not unlike Paul. He was only human.
The resources open to him are also available to us.

To lay aside weights is great advice. After a speech in Fayette-
ville, North Carolina, Brooks received a letter from a black
woman who had been in his audience. She had grown up in
Cotton Plant, Arkansas, she wrote, but had been living in North
Carolina for some years. She mentioned that for a long time
she had wanted to serve on a jury, but was never allowed to
because of her race. Now, times had changed, she had been
accepted on a panel, and was enjoying the experience as much
as she had thought she would. "But I don't hold any resentment!
I'm a grandmother now, and I've put the past behind me. I
just try to serve the age I'm in."

Such a wise and sensitive woman is a credit to our sex as
well as to her race.

Although he told us to covet earnestly the best gifts, one
thing Paul did not mention (I wish he had) was a sense of
humor. If we have it, we should cherish it; if not, we should
cultivate it, for it's one of the greatest assets and most precious
gifts—a blessing not only to the one who possesses it, but to
all who are fortunate enough to live and work with one who

does. It keeps us from taking ourselves too seriously. Disappointments and even failures won't get us down.

I read in a newspaper a little human interest story about a woman who did her washing by hand in the old way, and hung it out in the yard to dry. But it was such a big washing that the line broke, and the wet clothes came down with it. She washed them out again, and this time she spread them on the grass. But a big dog with muddy feet came along, and walked all over the damp clothes. When she went out to bring them in and wash them for the third time, she said to her neighbor, "Ain't it funny that he didn't miss nothin'?"

I'm afraid that instead of seeing anything funny in that situation, I would have howled!

That strange woman reminded me of Mrs. Wiggs of the Cabbage Patch. She was one of the delights of my childhood. Her creator, Alice C. Hegan Rice, called her a philosopher because she was always able to triumph over her trials and troubles. She viewed her world and its inhabitants through rose-colored spectacles. She was middle-aged, poor, undereducated, underprivileged, and undercultivated, but she had a sense of humor which never failed her. She was never sorry for herself, nor did she allow envy to make her miserable. She was one of the happiest women I ever knew. I say "knew," because whatever you say, I did know Mrs. Wiggs!

I admired her, too, for she had star quality.

2

Seeing with the Eyes of Love
(St. Valentine's Day)

In one of the old Greek myths, a young sculptor falls in love with the beautiful young girl he has created in marble. His prayers to the gods to make her a mortal are granted, and Galatea comes to life and makes the young Pygmalion happy. Galatea, so far as I ever heard, never asserted herself, or talked back, or in any way made Pygmalion regret his creative impulse.

If such a thing could happen outside a myth or fairy tale, I'm afraid the real-life young woman would have more spirit. George Bernard Shaw, in his witty play, *Pygmalion*, adapted the Greek theme to nineteenth century England. The play depicts a professor of speech who molds a bit of humanity in the rough—an east-end flower girl—into one who had the surface qualities of a "lady." Professor Higgins's interest in Eliza Doolittle was purely academic. A phonetics expert, he was concerned only with demonstrating to his friend, Colonel Pickering, that he could take the ignorant, unkempt flower girl with the horrible Cockney accent, and in six months teach her to speak with an English diction so perfect that they could pass her off as a duchess at an ambassador's garden party; or even, he said ironically, as a clerk or lady's maid. Colonel Pickering agreed to put up the money for the experiment, which would include a wardrobe for Eliza.

Professor Higgins worked Eliza like a slave. He bullied, threatened, bawled her out, flew into rages, and occasionally coaxed. Colonel Pickering, on the contrary, was unfailingly courteous and considerate, often protesting Professor Higgins's harsh treatment.

The occasion of Eliza's test arrived. She brilliantly fulfilled Professor Higgins's prediction; she was the sensation of the evening, producing an impression of remarkable distinction and beauty. The next day, in a conversation with Colonel Pickering, Eliza voiced her resentment against her mentor (act 5).

> *Liza* (to Pickering): . . . It was from you I learnt really nice manners; and that is what makes one a lady, isn't it? You see, it was so very difficult for me with the example of Professor Higgins always before me . . . using bad language on the slightest provocation. . . . But do you know what began my real education? . . . Your calling me "Miss Doolittle"—that day when I first came to Wimpole Street. That was the beginning of self-respect for me. And there were a hundred little things you never noticed, because they came naturally to you. Things about standing up, and taking off your hat and opening door[s]—
> *Pickering:* Oh, that was nothing.
> *Liza:* Yes: things that shewed you thought and felt about me as if I were something better than a scullery maid. . . . You see, really and truly, apart from the things anyone can pick up (the dressing, and the proper way of speaking, and so on), the difference between a lady and a flower girl is not how she behaves, but how she's treated. I shall always be a flower girl to Professor Higgins, because he always treats me as a flower girl, and always will; but I know I can be a lady to you, because you always treat me as a lady, and always will.

It would be a little surprising to find the young flower girl showing so much intellectual maturity and discernment in six months, were it not that she was the mouthpiece of George Bernard Shaw, who was a very discerning old gentleman. He suggests here an interesting point of view about the ugly and depressing aspects of life. He suggests a new and unusual way in which some of the responsibility for changing these conditions rests upon you and me, a way which has a relation to Keats's description of beauty—it's "in the eye of the beholder." The eye of the beholder does not create the beauty, but it may discern it; may seek it out and find it, even when it is not very obvious; in a sense it may even create it, by giving self-confidence, for admiration often brings a sparkle to the eye and a glow to the cheek. Flattery, though it does little credit to the one who consciously employs it, often becomes the truth. This applies to the human spirit as well. It has a way of measuring up to people's expectations, and responds quickly to warmth and understanding. Love has a transforming power which nothing else can equal.

Eliza's shrewd comments remind me of another conversation, one in which I took part. The owner of a garment factory, who is also a Christian, was talking to me one day about his interest in the working conditions of his women employees and his concern for their welfare. He related his experience with a foreman who had one serious failing—frequent use of profanity.

"I didn't know that until the women told me," said Mr. P., the owner. "I didn't lose any time doing something about it. I called him to my office after work. I began, 'How are you getting along?' The foreman, a young man, replied, 'Fine, I think. I'd like to know what *you* think of *me.*' "

Mr. P. said, "In some ways you're the best foreman I've ever had. I've never known anyone to learn the work so quickly. But you have one bad fault."

In obvious alarm, the young man said, "What is that?"

"You use a good deal of profanity. I don't like that, and my employees don't like it. You are working with ladies here, and your language should be that of a gentleman."

How much credit is reflected on the owner of that factory

by the fact that he saw his seamstresses not as inferiors or as women who had no standards, but as "ladies"! He considered it his responsibility to see that in his shop they were respected as such by himself and others. I have no doubt that Mr. P.'s treatment of them made ladies of any that, when they first came, might have fallen short of the requirements of that somewhat outmoded old word.

The young man, too, benefited by the high standards of his employer. Finding that he was expected to act like a gentleman, he did so. Then he took a further step; to Mr. P.'s surprise, he presented himself as a new member of the Sunday School class which his employer taught. In a book called the *Vantage Point* by Hilda Morris I remember a character with one of the most lovable traits I ever heard of—that of seeing things through the owner's eyes. "The spiritual and emotional value of objects was what registered with her," said the author. "She saw material things as they were intended to be seen." When her niece said, "What an awful hat Mrs. Balder had on!" she answered, "Was it? I scarcely noticed. Ellen Balder always was so happy and confident about her clothes, that even when they looked absurd one tried to see them as she did."

When a little neighbor boy brought her a bunch of wilting dandelions, she saw in them what he intended—a fragrant nosegay. She never scorned people's hopes and intentions which fell short of their mark; she looked upon their efforts with tenderness and understanding. Consequently, her very life was like a healing balm or a restoring elixir to those who knew her.

Is it too naïve to suggest that a simple but practical plan for putting more goodness and happiness into the world is to look at people with more understanding and tolerance and with less suspicion? When we get used to that much good will in ourselves, we can go farther; we can look at them with the eyes of love. Our world today is smarting from too much suspicion, too many charges of sin in others, too many evil thoughts. A turmoil of unrest and fear of each other has been stirred up in America. We actually seemed happier when we were at war. I think we were, for then we hated only our enemy. Now, we hate and fear ourselves. These emotions spread like dry rot in a barrel of apples; they have as harmful an effect on those who entertain them as on the objects of their suspicion. How badly we need a change from the evil eye to the eye of love!

"If thine eye be evil, thy whole body shall be full of darkness. If therefore the light that is in thee be darkness, how great is that darkness!" (Matt. 6:23).

Dr. Christian Norberg once told of an incident concerning a preacher he knew in Denmark. "He did what preachers like to do sometimes," said Dr. Norberg, "he told his congregation a thing or two. He got quite a number of things off his chest. Then he went proudly home to dinner, glorying in his own spunk. His wife, contrary to her habit, made no reference to the service. Finally, he asked her, 'What did you think of my sermon?'

"She hesitated a moment, then said, 'I missed the tears of Jesus. When he told people of their sins, he wept over them. He never sat in the seat of the scornful.' "

Perhaps one reason why Jesus' life was such a great constructive force is that he not only looked for the best and found it in everyone he encountered, but he even saw what they might become! He frequently saw in them traits they did not know they possessed. The classic example is Peter. I think the surprise of that week, in Galilee, must have been Jesus' calling the impulsive, somewhat unstable Simon a rock! But from that day on, Simon struggled to become what the Master expected of him. How well he succeeded in sloughing off the old character and assuming the new is shown by the fact that his real name was dropped in favor of his nickname. And when a wonderful cathedral was built in Rome and named for him, it was called not St. Simon's, but St. Peter's.

Jesus certainly saw something in the woman of Samaria which his disciples, shocked and disapproving when they found him conversing with her, would not have seen. Maybe she had a good mind—a native intelligence. Anyway, Jesus told this alien woman, from whose hands no Pharisee would have even accepted a cup of water, a thing he had told no other soul—that he was the Messiah. His conversation with her is one of the most interesting and revealing talks recorded in the New Testament.

He saw something in the rich young ruler of the synagogue which makes me very curious. It was not what the world saw; I am sure of that. The young man had wealth and position; these were apparent in his appearance. Quite possibly he had talent and charm. The disciples would have loved having him in the Master's school; he would have raised the prestige of the whole business immeasurably. Since anyone could see those things, I think it was something else that Jesus saw when he "looked at him and loved him." He saw something that young man could become; a nobility which he might attain in the kingdom of God. But the young ruler passed on, and Jesus with saddened heart watched him go, for he never forced anyone into his Way; and the young man is immortalized only by his failure to perceive greatness in another.

Jesus saw potentialities in each of his disciples, most of whom changed the direction of their lives and grew greatly in spirit.

The rehabilitation of Mary Magdalene, apparently as simple as it was sudden, proves that people respond in kind to the way in which they are treated. Jesus treated her with respect, and consequently she became respectable.

The Pharisees who did not like Jesus said he had a liking for "low company." The truth is, he never recognized any company as "low." Each individual had his own status. Jesus looked at each one with loving eyes and saw him as a child of God.

Most of us do not follow Jesus in this respect, just as we do not follow him in most others. It is difficult, certainly. Let us think what it means: Suppose he came to your city and let a committee of officials and bankers and Rotarians wait while he had a long talk with a Negro. Suppose he said to some prominent churchmen, "Publicans and harlots will go into heaven before you." You see? Shocking, isn't it? It's because we have so little true humility. We prefer our own pompous standards to those of God.

A woman called a Washington minister on the phone to berate him for allowing blacks to come to an interchurch meeting. He answered, "But what we are doing is simple Christianity." And the woman said, "Well, you can go along with Christianity only so far." That ended the conversation, as he laughed at her manifest absurdity, and she hung up in a huff.

I heard a radio commentator who has a large audience refer to communists as "vermin." Would Jesus want us to see them as vermin? Or as misguided human beings who have been trained in wrong ideas? There is a Sanskrit quotation which reads: "The world will be destroyed, also the mighty ocean will dry up; and this broad earth will be consumed. Therefore, sirs, cultivate friendliness, cultivate compassion."

If we could see with the omniscience of God into the background, the heredity, and environment of those who somehow get at cross purposes with society, we would put the blame frequently on society. A deathless old poem, "The Bridge of Sighs," by Thomas Hood about a pitiful derelict who had thrown herself into the river, continues to indict each generation for its failures:

> Pick her up tenderly,
> Lift her with care;
> Fashion'd so slenderly,
> Young, and so fair!

Pity for the unfortunate, when it is too late to do anything to help, comes easily. I think God expects much more of us Christians than a facile tear or a mournful croak over the sad state of the world. I think he expects us to do something about it. So many people, instead of creating, are busy destroying; if not through hate, through indifference. The ultimate in lack of understanding was the remark made by the farmer, as they took his wife to the insane asylum.

He stood in the door watching, and said to a neighbor, "I can't figure what set her off. She ain't been out of the house in twenty years."

Human nature has a way of measuring up to expectations. My mother used to say, "Anyone who praises my cooking can make me work myself to death. I don't have a grain of sense!"

It's an arresting thought that if situations or people do not please us, the cure may be in ourselves!

When I was a girl, one of my favorite romances was a tale set in England in the twelfth century—*The White Ladies of Worcester* by Florence L. Barclay. The most delightful character in it was a silver-haired Catholic bishop named Symon of Worcester. He was a great lover of beauty, and he always drank when at the table from a goblet of ruby glass, pouring his drink from a Venetian glass pitcher.

His guests sometimes wondered what choice kind of wine the bishop kept for his own use. If they asked, he told them. "The kind used at the marriage feast at Cana in Galilee, when the supply of an inferior quality had failed. This, my friends, is pure water, wholesome, refreshing, and not costly. I drink it from a glass which is the color of grape juice, partly in order that my guests may not feel chilled . . . partly because I enjoy the emblem.

"The gifts of circumstance, life and nature vary," he said, "not so much in themselves, as in the human vessels which contain them. If the heart be a ruby goblet, the humblest form of pure love filling it will assume the rich tint and fervor of romance. If the mind be in itself a thing of vivid tints and glowing colors, the dullest thought within it will take on a lustre, a sparkle, a glow of brilliancy. Thus, when men or matters seem to me dull or wearisome, to myself I say, 'Symon! Thou art this day thyself a pewter pot.' "

Then the bishop would fill up his goblet and hold it to the light.

"Aye, the best wine!" he would say. " 'Thou hast kept the best wine until now.' The water of earth, drawn by faithful servants acting in unquestioning obedience to the commands of Jesus, transmitted by the word and power of the Divine Son, outpoured for others in loving service—this is ever 'the best wine.' "*

How comforting it is to think that Jesus looks at each of us with the eyes of love. We are not dull pewter pots to him. Instead of our mistakes and failures, he sees our hopes, our aspirations. He takes note of each uplift of our hearts. He sees in us potentialities for better things—the finer, nobler men and women we could become.

*Florence L. Barclay, *The White Ladies of Worcester* (New York: G. P. Putnam's Sons, 1917), pp. 8–9.

I think that I shall never see
A poem lovely as a tree.
JOYCE KILMER

And he shall be like a tree
planted by the rivers of water,
that bringeth forth his fruit in his season.
PSALM 1:3

3

Trees with Biblical Significance
(Arbor Day)

When I was a very small school child I was introduced, as it were, to trees. Until then I had been no more conscious of them than of the roof over my head. But my first grade teacher told the class that March was tree-planting time, and we were taken to the schoolyard to watch the planting of a small sapling. This was done with a small ceremony.

Our "art work" (an admittedly flattering term) for a few weeks was concerned with leaves of various kinds and drawing trees, both denuded and fully clothed. Our daily singing session frequently included the song that begins, "Miss April gave a party. The leaves by hundreds came. . . ."

I became so saturated with the importance and beauty of trees that I have never lost my admiration and affection for them. Perhaps this arboreal background makes it impossible for me to think of some biblical characters apart from certain trees. A juniper tree recalls Elijah, and suggests defeatism. The palm tree reminds me of Deborah, a wise woman dispensing justice. A sycamore brings to mind an unhappy little rich man whose

27

28   SIMPLE TALKS FOR SPECIAL DAYS

life was changed by the circumstance of his climbing a tree.

Do you, too, make the same mental connections? There are some others—the barren fig tree, for example, which Jesus used as an object lesson; the oak, whose branches proved Absolom's undoing. The author of the first Psalm said a tree—any strong, healthy tree—reminded him of a righteous man, upstanding and straight, proudly holding his head high because he's never had to bend it in shame. How he would have appreciated Joyce Kilmer's lines: "A tree that looks at God all day, And lifts her leafy arms to pray."

When we think of a palm tree we may think of a number of pleasant things—the blue Pacific, southern Florida, the beach at Waikiki, a full moon. But if we turn our minds toward biblical trees, a palm suggests to me one person only, a woman, Deborah.

"And Deborah, a prophetess, the wife of Lapidoth, she judged Israel at that time. And she dwelt under the palm tree of Deborah . . . and the children of Israel came up to her for judgment" (Judges 4:4,5).

There are two considerations about what happened under that palm tree that should give us a thrill of pride.

The first and most important is that the Hebrews, who are our spiritual ancestors, believed in justice and dispensed it, or tried to. The Greeks, who had a finer culture in all things except religion, were not even approaching their Golden Age; and when they finally did, their religion was still completely pagan. Their gods were so dissolute and malicious and whimsical, so *human*, that most of the Greek intelligentsia had been turned off and believed in nothing. Why shouldn't we be just as proud of spiritual ancestors as of physical ones? We acknowledge Jesus as Savior and Lord, and we cannot dispute the beautiful tribute of Rabbi Enlow: "We see in Jesus all that is best and most divine in the life of Israel, the Eternal People, whose child he was." It makes no sense for Christians to try to separate Jesus from his origins and to deny the powerful influence of his history on his own life and teachings. Antisemitism is as unintelligent as it is un-Christian.

Justice is a religious concept; the Hebrews, the people with the clearest and best understanding of God and of the inherent rights of the individual, were the first to begin dispensing justice—not just to the upper class, the rich and powerful, but to the humble people as well. I don't know what kind of palm Deborah sat under. Presumably it was one that provided shade. But regardless of that, the symbol of justice should be a tall royal palm, one that would rise above self-interest, sectionalism, prejudice, and pressures from all the special interests that cause miscarriages of justice.

As I was walking home past the Supreme Court Building one spring day, I saw a young black woman, surrounded by a group of children, all the same size, mostly black. I think she was a schoolteacher pointing out to her class one of the sights of Washington. She was pointing to the front of the building and seemed to be reading something. Because of traffic noises I couldn't hear what she said, but I wondered if she were reading the motto over the great doors, "Equal Justice Under Law," and how she would explain that to her black pupils.

The second thrilling fact about Deborah is that a woman was chosen to be a judge. Her wisdom and strength of character must have been impressive, for she succeeded in a man's job. Obviously, she was concerned about justice and so identified with the pursuit of it that no other choice seemed as fitting. It was a responsible position, and therefore Deborah was honored by being chosen.

A character in the play *The Madwoman of Chaillot* by Jean Giradoux says, "There's nothing wrong with the world a sensible woman couldn't put right in an afternoon."

An extravagant claim, even if it had been made by a twentieth-century Women's Libber! But none of them would make it, because the obvious retort would be, "Well, why hasn't she

done it? Aren't there any sensible women?" Perhaps it was the
Madwoman herself who said that! I have heard it said that if
the Baptists and Methodists of the South had acted together,
they could have solved our social problems there long ago. I
believe that if the missionary societies of those two denominations
were to act jointly now, with devotion and dedication, tensions
and injustices based on sexual, racial and religious differences
could be wiped out.

In America since women got the franchise I believe they have
generally put the weight of their influence on the side of justice.
But I know the job hasn't yet been finished. There is still work
to do. Long after Deborah judged Israel under the palm, Isaiah
said about the servant of God, "He will not fail or be discouraged
till he has established justice in the earth" (Isa. 42:4, RSV). And
we cannot rest until this is accomplished.

When I think of a juniper tree I think of Elijah. You may
remember that Elijah was frightened so badly by a woman that
he ran for his life. He fled from his country, Israel, and went
down into Judea; he even "went a day's journey into the wilderness," and didn't feel safe even then! True, Jezebel was a mean
and vicious woman who would stop at nothing. One can sympathize with Elijah even while acknowledging that he wasn't acting
much like a hero. He realized himself that he was giving a good
imitation of a coward, for he flopped down under that juniper
tree and prayed to die. "It is enough; now, O Lord, take my
life; for I am not better than my fathers" (1 Kings 19:4).

It is a salutary experience for anyone to come to the conclusion
that he (or she) is not as superior to others as he had thought.
Elijah's prayer was not granted, for which I'm sure he was thankful later. We make a distinction, as we should, between God's
answering prayers and granting our requests. If Elijah felt his
prayer was not answered, it was probably because God couldn't
get his attention just then; all Elijah's attention was centered
on himself. I imagine that condition has always been an effective
bar to hearing God's voice.

A few days later, God said to him, "What doest thou here, Elijah?" (1 Kings 19:9).

Don't you love the imagery of those ancient writers? Such a spiritual experience was so very real to them that they described it in simple everyday terms, as if a conversation with God was the most natural thing in the world! In more literal twentieth-century language, we say that Elijah's conscience was beginning to stir—an experience common to all of us.

He answered defensively: "I have been very jealous for the Lord God of hosts: for the children of Israel have forsaken thy covenant, thrown down thine altars, and slain thy prophets with the sword; and I, even I only, am left; and they seek my life, to take it away" (1 Kings 19:10).

After giving Elijah an object lesson, to show him that he (God) was not in the sound and fury and destructive activity of the wind, earthquake and fire, God responded to Elijah's self-justification and self-pity: "Yet I have left me seven thousand in Israel, all the knees which have not bowed unto Baal, and every mouth which hath not kissed him" (1 Kings 19:18).

I think that lesson was one of the great milestones in man's spiritual education, when a prophet realized that the voice of God is to be heard only in moments of quietude and calm, and that one has to listen for it. A line of poetry which I remember but cannot place reads: "I heard the booming sunset gun, I did not hear the sun go down." The gun was man's device. The sun is God's.

Another great lesson God taught Elijah out there in the wilderness concerned the importance—or unimportance—of numbers. "Never underestimate your opponent" is a well-known bit of political and military wisdom. It is also a mistake to underrate your colleagues. Elijah panicked because he underestimated the number of faithful in Israel and their potential power.

True, they were a minority. Ahab the king and the heathen princess he had married had debauched the court, and most of the kingdom had gone along, willingly or unwillingly. The king's party was a huge majority. But God was on the side of the minority, which became seven thousand plus one, and that changed the odds.

One of the earliest lessons learned in Sunday School is that what God wants is devotion and consecration, not just numbers. We learned it in stories like Gideon and the three hundred men carefully chosen to fight against the Midianites who were "as the grasshoppers for multitude," and like Abraham bargaining with God for Sodom. A little core of ten incorruptible men could have saved the city. It was Abraham who gave up at that point, not God.

It seems that some of our modern religious leaders have forgotten those old lessons. My husband (generally a mild-mannered man with a high boiling point) sometimes explodes when he reads the ads of some churches on Saturday morning which make a point of the large number they always have in Sunday School. "They're everlastingly preoccupied with numbers!" he exclaims at the breakfast table. "They concentrate on getting people there, and don't give enough attention to what they give them after they get them there!"

When he was president of the Southern Baptist Convention, he used to say in speeches, "Let's have a moratorium on numbers for awhile and think more about the quality of our teaching."

God seldom has a majority to work with, but there is always the symbolic seven thousand plus one. And somehow, as the years pass, the ideals of the minorities become the ideas of the majorities. And that is God's doing, too.

There are lots of sycamore trees, so that word does not necessarily take us back to a scene described by Luke. But a sycamore tree growing in Jericho does make us think of the little man who wasn't in the crowd because he had climbed the tree, the better to see Jesus.

This story has always reminded me of circus day in Fort Smith when I was a schoolchild. The circus came south at the end of summer when it was still comfortable to be outside in a tent.

The sun would be hot, but there was a special feeling in the air, a hint that fall was on the way. Summer vacation had ended and the school year had begun, but our school principals had all been boys once, so each year all schools were dismissed in the morning for the parade. And we were even allowed to straggle back in the afternoon, for the parade was always late. I was half-grown before I got to see the performance in the Big Top, but the parade was so satisfying I never felt deprived.

There was just one drawback for me. Unless I could get to the curb and stand in front of everyone, I couldn't see a thing. Many a time I wished I were six feet tall! We didn't have any trees on Garrison Avenue, our main street, and even if we had I doubt if I could have climbed one.

The day Jesus of Nazareth, the eloquent young preacher, came to Jericho the whole town turned out to see him. Zacchaeus realized he wouldn't be able to see and hear without some eleva- tion, so he ran ahead and clambered up a tree. This opportunity was obviously very important to him. Jesus was a celebrity! Stories about him had traveled by the grapevine. Zacchaeus, having heard them, was intrigued and wanted to see this Jesus. Human nature was no different then. Jesus was popular. Crowds loved and followed him. No one followed Zacchaeus, in spite of his money and position and the power it gave him. No one clamored to be with him or loved him. In fact, he was a very unpopular man in the community, for he was a chief of the publicans or tax gatherers. He had set up his headquarters in Jericho, a good location, for it lay on the road which led from Berea to Judea and Egypt. It was a detestable city, as unpopular as a town as Zacchaeus was as a man. And oddly enough, the sycamore was an unpopular tree! It was the fig tree of Palestine, but the fruit was so insipid that only the very poor ate it. It was a sycamore fig that Jesus "cursed." An unpopular man in an unpopular town climbed an unpopular tree. Just an unpopular mess!

But this was the most important act he ever performed in his life, and that reflected importance on the tree. Luke says plainly, it was a sycamore tree, giving the tree full credit, and so it went into the record and down in history. When I think of a sycamore tree, I think of Zacchaeus, and when I think of Zacchaeus, I think of a sycamore tree. The two are inseparable.

None of the disciples changed his ways and purposes as suddenly as Zacchaeus did. His whole outlook changed completely and utterly and immediately. He made the most important decision of his life and put it into effect at once. By announcing it in the presence of witnesses, he made it almost impossible to back out. "Lord, the half of my goods I give to the poor; and if I have taken any thing from any man by false accusation, I restore him fourfold" (Luke 19:8).

That was the measure of sincerity. His conversion cost him something, but he paid it joyfully. The value of a sentiment or ideal is the sacrifice we are willing to make for it.

Zacchaeus's impulse to give Jesus something, and without delay, was very natural. How intelligent of him to realize that the best thing he could give was his own reformation. There was so much good in Zacchaeus! But it wasn't organized. What he needed was a worthy purpose and ideal at the center of his life. A shrine. Someone to love and worship and obey, and he found all these when he found Jesus. All in all, it was the greatest day in his life—the day he forgot his dignity and climbed a tree.

There's a universality about this story. It is not limited by time or place. Zacchaeus has lived in many countries. He lives in America today, and so does Mrs. Zacchaeus! I think we can guess that there was a sense of inferiority in this little man which made him aggressive. It may have led him to become a publican, hoping to gain prestige through wealth. But it did not work that way. Many a man has thought wealth would open all doors, only to find it does not. Of course, every rich man has sycophants and hangers-on by the dozens, but it must be cold comfort to realize the attraction may be his favors. At some time the fun goes out of the game for even the most successful player.

I believe Zacchaeus may have reached this point, and when he met Jesus the scales fell from his eyes, and the illusion of his own importance was swept away. That, too, is a universal experience.

I liked Zacchaeus for climbing that tree; it showed he wasn't a stuffed shirt. I liked him even better for the promptness with which he acted as he climbed down without shilly-shallying or hesitating. Sometimes we have to go down in order to go up. I like the symbolism—he got up above the traffic of life, the throng of people, the press of activities. When he did that, he saw Jesus' face. And he fell like a ripe plum!

How excited he must have been when Jesus said, "Make haste and come down, Zacchaeus. I want to dine with you today." I think Jesus was probably smiling when he spoke to Zacchaeus, as one can laugh at a friend caught in an undignified position. I'm sure his eyes were warm and friendly. And Zacchaeus was won completely. He did make haste, and joyfully conducted Jesus to his house.

And I suspect that Jesus had a lot more fun there than he would have had at some other places, the rich young ruler's, for instance. I imagine there were many laughing references to the host's choice of a vantage point. But I think Zacchaeus enjoyed it all. He had made some friends. And I know, just as well as if I'd been there, that Zacchaeus found himself that day, too, and was never the same again.

There is a legend which gives us a brief sequel. It says that shortly after Zacchaeus's meeting with Jesus, his wife saw him slip out of the house at dawn. When he came back he said nothing about where he had been. A few days later it happened again. And then there was a third time. This time she followed. He got tools and a water jar from the barn, and filled the jar at the well. Then he went to a tree on the outskirts of the

village. There he raked away brush and leaves, leaving the sur-
roundings neat. He pruned the dead leaves, watered the roots,
and was patting the trunk lovingly when she came up. He didn't
seem surprised or embarrassed. He just said, "This is the tree
I was in when I met him." It had become a sacred spot.

No life is complete without such a shrine, a holy of holies,
a sacred place. Or as a teacher of mine once quoted: "Keep a
green bough in thy heart and God will send thee a singing
bird."

Do not pray for tasks equal to your powers.
Pray for powers equal to your tasks.
PHILLIPS BROOKS

4

The Conquering Cross
(Palm Sunday)

Because the central symbol of the Christian faith is a cross, and its motto or slogan (for want of a better word) is "In This Sign Conquer," I have marshaled my thoughts along the line of the conquering cross.

Many of us accepted this concept without question when we were children. But to a mature person, learning about it for the first time, it must seem almost incredible that such an ugly, rough object could be elevated to a place of sacred reverence. An object, moreover, that for many centuries has stood for shame, disgrace, and the most degrading failure.

But when Jesus chose death upon it in preference to life on the world's terms, he changed the meaning: that symbol of death and failure became a symbol of victory—victory of the human spirit over physical pain, betrayal, defeat and even death.

We owe the motto to Constantine, a Roman soldier (A.D. 288–337) who wanted to be emperor of Rome. He became a Christian as the result of a dream in which he saw a flaming cross in the sky, accompanied by the words, *"in hoc signo vinces."*

He had been fighting for some years with several other aspi-
rants to the throne of Rome, and he undoubtedly saw this vision
as a promise of military victory. After winning a decisive battle
he became Emperor Constantine the First, also known as Constantine the Great.

This victory had one result far more important than any earthly
status or prestige for Constantine. It secured safety and tolerance
for Christians throughout the empire—a very welcome change
in their condition. This protection was made official by the Edict
of Milan.

Some years later, Constantine made Christianity the official
religion of the empire. He decided it would be helpful to get
completely away from the paganism of Rome and found a new
capital. So he had another dream (or so he said!) that told him
Byzantium would be the best place, and so that city, which
became known as Constantinople, was for awhile the capital
of the Roman Empire.

So Constantine has always enjoyed an exalted position in Christian church history. He was probably the first Christian of note
and power, and that fact helped establish the still infant religion
on a firm foundation.

Unfortunately, his moral qualities did not, and never would,
make him great. God was able to use him, as he uses so many
who are not saints but very human beings. He was a military
conqueror, like Alexander, who was also called "The Great."
Both lived by the sword. It is strange to think that the man
who gave us this wonderful uplifting motto did not understand
the implications of it from the point of view of the One who
went to the cross. He failed to understand that the victory is
not won on a battlefield but over self. Nor did he understand
that the way of the Cross is not the way of worldly honors
but the way of sacrifice.

It has been pointed out many times that Jesus did not go
to the cross for commenting on the brilliance of the lilies of
the field or even for healing the sick. He was crucified for med-

dling in the religious and political issues of his day. To the priests he was a dangerous radical; to the Romans, a potential subversive. I don't think we can remind ourselves too often that he was not a conformist. He was undaunted by tradition.

Some people seem to have a misconception about what constitutes one's cross—that it is any burden one can't get rid of. A woman made a bid for equal status when she said to her pastor, after listening to his sermon on Palm Sunday, "I have my cross, too—I suffer from boils."

How quickly she would have laid down that cross if she could! And why not? What earthly good would be served by her putting up with them? Paul referred to his ailment as a thorn in his side. He never called it his cross.

Jesus' cross was altogether different. It was *our* "boils" he bore—our burdens, our sins—and he took them on himself of his own free will. He had a choice.

Let's look at some of the details of the trial which condemned him to death. It was a hollow mockery, the most complete travesty of justice. My father-in-law, who was a distinguished lawyer in Arkansas, was often called on to give a lecture which he called, "The Trial of Jesus from a Lawyer's Viewpoint." He had worked it out from the Gospels and some histories. He showed how a few rulers of the synagogue (which was controlled by one sect of the Jews, perhaps comparable to the John Birch Society), in their haste to get Jesus convicted and out of their way, had broken their own laws as if they were so many worthless eggshells. Yet they had fostered and maintained a religion which was concerned mainly with obeying laws.

Their law required that trials be held in the official Sanhedrin building. They went to another place. Their law expressly forbade trials at night. They held this one at night. There could be only one reason for both those infractions—their need for secrecy. They met while a Jewish feast, the Passover, was in progress. That was also forbidden. If the verdict was that death was to be asked for (of Rome), at least one night must elapse before the execution. It's shocking enough that only one night was allowed for the sake of possible errors. This time they did not wait even one night.

The law said the Sanhedrin was to be polled individually, each member rendering his own verdict. This was not done. Was Caiaphas unwilling to risk a "not guilty" from someone? Gamaliel, perhaps?

In this illegal and maneuvered setting, Caiaphas began to call the witnesses they had assembled, and what a spectacle that was! The witnesses, who did not really know what they were talking about, as we can see from Mark's account, couldn't agree with each other. Although they had been coached, they messed things up, while the high priest got madder and madder. Another bunch was brought in who had heard something, or been told something, about the temple being destroyed by Jesus and being rebuilt, all in three days, but they distorted that. You remember that what he had said was on an occasion when he was in Jerusalem with his disciples, and some of them were exclaiming about the beautiful buildings, and Jesus said, "Do you see these great buildings? There will not be left here one stone upon another, that will not be thrown down" (Mark 13:2, RSV). Of course it happened exactly as he said. But Jesus did not do it.

Caiaphas, who had probably expected the proceedings to go off as if on greased wheels and was very likely fuming by this time, said furiously to Jesus, "Well! Haven't you anything to say to that?" Jesus had not, and didn't need to. The silly lies of the hired accusers fell under the weight of their own stupidity.

So, after all the trouble the rulers had gone to, and the laws they had broken, they still had nothing to convict him on, not enough to impress the Sanhedrin, let alone Rome! So the high priest, in a kind of desperation, broke yet another law. The law said a man must not be asked to incriminate himself. The high priest, well aware of that, yet said to Jesus, "Are you the Christ, the Son of the Blessed?" (Mark 14:61, RSV).

If Jesus had remained silent, as he had every right to do, he might have escaped with his life. But without hesitating a moment, he answered, "I am: and ye shall see the Son of man sitting on the right hand of power, and coming in the clouds of heaven" (Mark 14:62). With those words he signed his death warrant. But the decision to take that step had been made in the Garden of Gethsemane or even earlier. He knew that he was not going to deny his mission, his messiahship, when it eventually came to a showdown. He didn't go to meet it; he didn't court martyrdom. I suspect he had hoped for more years of teaching. But when the crisis came, he was spiritually prepared and ready.

Should we say, then, that Jesus chose death that night rather than life? Long, long before, Moses had said to his people in the wilderness, "I have set before you life and death, blessing and cursing: therefore choose life" (Deut. 30:19). That is one of the most beautifully dramatic statements of the two contrasting courses offered human beings, yet it was expressed in a primitive society that was still groping, almost blindly, after a spiritual God.

If Moses could have been present in that Jerusalem trial room, and Jesus, a young man, had turned to the aged hero of his people for strength and encouragement, would Moses have said again, "Choose life"? I think he would, and that is what Jesus chose. For life means something more than consciousness, a heart beating, a pulse throbbing. That is merely existence. Jesus did give up the brief earthly tenure of the body. He gave up life in the physical shell for the sake of an enduring one. He chose life in its broadest, most inclusive sense. He gave up a narrow self-centered period of personal aims in exchange for a brilliant triumphant ascent to his heavenly home and eternal fellowship with his Father.

Sir Philip Sidney is one of the romantic and glamorous figures of history. His name stands for chivalry and courtesy. After being wounded in battle he gave his cup of water, all he had, to a private soldier, saying that this fellow needed it more. Sidney subsequently died from his wound. Historians say that although he suffered a great deal of pain, "his first thought was always for the discomfort he caused those who nursed him." He was a poet, and a "gentil knight." His last poem, written just before he died of the wound in his thigh, began, "Magnificently I take leave of all transitory things." He was no mean follower of the One who gave us the perfect example of the surrender of transitory for permanent things. Yet Sidney's death was accidental and involuntary. Jesus' death was his own choice.

Don Marquis in *The Dark Hours* pictures Lazarus when he realizes Jesus is going to be crucified. In that instant a great truth dawned on Lazarus—as Don Marquis imagined it—and quietly but with utter conviction he said, "What is death to him?"

Jesus chose to pass through the experience of death for our sakes. The consequent difference this has made to Christians— the reduction of our fears of it—was expressed in a very illuminating way by C. S. Lewis in a news magazine as he wrote of the death of a friend whom he loved and revered, a contemporary from whom he learned much: "No event has so corroborated my faith in the next world as Williams did, simply by dying. When the idea of death and the idea of Williams thus met in my mind, it was the idea of death that was changed." Jesus changed the idea of death for us all just by dying for us, for in so doing he chose life in its richest, truest, and most eternal sense.

It was Judas who chose death, death of the soul. One of the most penetrating things ever said about him was, "It was not Christ Judas sold—it was himself." I used to think Jesus must have been terribly hurt at Judas's betrayal, but it would be much more like him to suffer because of what Judas did to himself.

It is a great temptation at this season to condemn everybody except ourselves—the Jewish sect who planned his death, the Romans who acceded to it, Judas who betrayed him, the mob who turned against him, the disciples who failed him, Pilate who washed his hands. Without even realizing it, today's Christians may subconsciously think, "Well, *we* didn't do it." Or even, shedding all possible guilt by association, "*I* didn't do it."

In the Gospel of Mark (chapter 14), the author includes a string of unworthy human traits which played their part in the arrest, trial and death of Jesus: insolence, violence, falsehood, blind hatred, brutality. Even the disciples were guilty of cowardice, flight, reliance on force, overconfidence and pettiness. Dr. Henry Sloan Coffin former president of Union Theological Seminary in New York says all of these and more are still with us and he names some of them: religious intolerance, bigotry, prejudice, unfaithfulness, mob spirit, militarism, public apathy, political expediency. These are our sins, and because of them he is still being rejected today.

The English essayist Thomas Carlyle was a very peppery old gentleman, not given to pulling his punches. One Sunday after church, a woman acquaintance irritated Carlyle with a very self-righteous comment on the sermon. She shook her head over the wickedness of the Jews, and added, "How delighted we would have been to throw our doors open to him, and to listen to his divine precepts. Do you not think so, Mr. Carlyle?"

He let her have it: "No, madam, I do not. I think had he come very fashionably dressed with plenty of money, preaching doctrines palatable to the higher orders, I might have had the honor of receiving from you a card of invitation on which was written, 'To meet our Savior.' But if he had come associating with publicans and those of the lower orders, *as he did*, you would have treated him as the Jews did, and cried, 'Take him to Newgate and hang him!'"

If Jesus had just been content to do a little good every day, spread a little sunshine, contribute to a few worthy charities, give his old clothes to the Salvation Army, brighten up the corner where he was, he might have had a nice long life like Methuselah. The writer of Genesis (5:27) tells us, "And all the days of Methuselah were nine hundred and sixty and nine years: and he died."

Dorothy Parker, hearing of the death of a political person who had managed to stay out of all controversies and avoid connection with all issues, asked, "How can they tell?" A good question.

The way of the Cross. We talk and sing about it with great ease, but do we really walk in it? And how can people tell?

God has set eternity in our hearts.
ECCLESIASTES 3:11
(as paraphrased by Clovis Chappell, D.D.)

5

Living on Sunrise
(Easter)

A few years ago my husband and I were in New York, and we went to see a play called, *On a Clear Day You Can See Forever.*

Easter is just such a day, no matter what the weather is like—a day that helps us to see "forever"—or eternity. It's like a spiritual telescope that gives us such a long-range view that the "intimations of immortality" which are all around us, but which we often fail to perceive because of the fogs and mists of daily living, come into focus, and we feel reassured about the existence of that heavenly home and its many mansions.

I once heard Dr. John Inzer, a Southern Baptist preacher, talk amusingly about his hometown in Alabama. He said that as the white people built up the town, they had pushed the blacks out to the periphery. As it happens, the town is ringed by hills, so the blacks got the beauty spots, and the white people succeeded in huddling down in the hollow. The blacks have given some interesting and beautiful names to their hills. One day Dr. Inzer heard his yardman, Robert, talking to a passing friend.

"Hello, Robert. How are you?"

"I'm fine. How's all your folks?"

"They're fine. Where you livin' now?"

"I live on the Moon Ridge."

"Where's your son livin'?"

"He lives on the edge of the Moon. Where you livin' at?"

"I live on Sunrise myself."

And then, in the rich warm tones of deep feeling, Dr. Inzer commented, "If the Reds should ever take over this country, and assign me ten acres and a broken-down mule, I would be ashamed of myself if I did not dwell on Sunrise and greet the dawn with a song!"

I was listening to this on a hot July day, but suddenly it seemed like Easter! Those last words of his sounded like a trumpet call bidding the world to rejoice because this is God's world, and he lives and reigns.

I don't believe it is possible to be a first-class pessimist and a first-class Christian at the same time.

I once knew a preacher who spent a great deal of time at the wailing wall. There was much more despair than hope in his sermons until one Sunday when he delivered a splendid line, "No man can believe in the sovereignty of God and not believe in the ultimate supremacy of righteousness." It impressed him so much that he converted himself—and that's not bad preaching!

We have a friend in Little Rock who is the worst worrier I ever saw. He worries about personal affairs and the state of the nation, impartially. He likes to talk to Brooks because he is calm, reasonable and reassuring. So whenever they are together, which is usually at dinner, he starts in on the most staggering questions, like, "How soon do you look for World War III? What are we going to do about Russia? Don't you think she outsmarts us? Are we going to give away the secret of the bomb?"

His wife usually tries to head him off. One evening on our

last visit, I remember she said, "Jack, don't start that now. Wait for the coffee."

His answer was, "Now, Jane, let me alone. I don't get to talk to Brooks much, and he makes me feel so good."

Brooks wasn't able to change anything, but Jack just liked to lean over and look through his eyes. Brooks looked through eyes of hope and faith. Jack had been exposed to similar influences all his life; he could have interpreted events and circumstances for himself—he wasn't stupid—and banished some of his own gloom. But he found it easier to worry.

It is true that the world is in a sorry state. I'm forever screaming silently, *What's the matter with everybody?* Most of us are confused and uncertain and often afraid. Two noted historians, Sorokin and Toynbee, have called this "a time of troubles." Is it possible for the sunrise of faith to gild this world of fears and shadows? But that's the whole point! "Living on sunrise" is not a matter of favorable circumstances, but of looking at circumstances through the eyes of faith; of having a margin of confidence and trust over and above the worst life can do. And nothing can give us this confidence except faith in a personal God and a risen Redeemer.

Christians should be the world's greatest optimists—not unthinking optimists, complacent, lazy, indifferent in the face of problems to be solved; but willing to tackle the problems unhampered by defeatism or the fear that nothing will do any good. They must believe, especially in these difficult times, that God controls in the affairs of men, that failure and defeat are never final, and that all things do work together for eventual good. Those who hold this ideal help to release a great constructive force in the world.

The late Bishop Angus Dun of Washington Cathedral, in his Easter message for Cathedral Age one spring, wrote: "Through the year, the church is slowly reciting her faith, but many come late. Many do not come in time for that majestic beginning, 'I believe in God, the Father Almighty.' Many do not come in time for the confession, 'I believe in Jesus Christ, our Lord and Savior.' Nor in time for the testimony, 'I believe in the Holy Spirit, God's living daily presence with us.' They arrive only in time for the last sentence, 'I believe in the life to come.' "

The implication is that they choose to believe in life after death for their own peace of mind in this life. But to limit one's religion to that one tenet is not only to make it a narrow and self-serving faith, for immortality concerns only the individual, but to disconnect it from this life, and that won't do. For to quote Bishop Dun again, "Easter cannot stand alone. We cannot separate what we shall be from what we are now."

All of us experience in our lives the death of many things before the ultimate adventure—death of the body. The death of hopes—haven't we all known that? Of desires, perhaps. Of belief in someone. Some have even known the bitterness of the death of love. Jesus' victory over death, in which we see proof of our own immortality, has also a promise for this life, for it is our signal that the cross of despair and disappointment, the grave of hopes, the tomb of love, may be transmitted into something strangely enriching and productive. The stone may be rolled away if our faith and love and self-forgetfulness are great enough, and our hopes may rise again from the wreckage to give us greater happiness than we had believed possible.

In 1958, after Brooks was defeated for reelection to Congress, he received many messages of sympathy. Among them was a congratulatory telegram. When Brooks opened it, he thought, "Well, this poor fellow has misread the returns!" Then he read the message. It said, "Jesus constantly made the point that we gain by giving, we win by losing, we live by dying. Congratulations on your victory."

Brooks carried that wire around in his pocket for months, and literally wore it out reading it!

Peter could tell us some poignant things about death in life.

Could anyone have experienced keener mental suffering than he must have from the time of Jesus' arrest until he knew he was forgiven? It is thought that in asking his question "Do you love me?" three times, Jesus was giving Peter three chances to wipe out his denials. Maybe so, but words are easily said. I think more likely it was to impress on Peter that he was not to indulge himself by a prolonged bout of self-pity, lamenting his own failures—a course which would nullify his potential usefulness and could conceivably destroy him.

So three times Jesus said, "If you love me, you must feed my sheep and lambs. *You must go to work.*" Love brings responsibilities. Love isn't something we say—it's something we do. That's just what Peter needed to show him that he was forgiven— the knowledge that he was not excluded from Jesus' plans. There is real comfort to be found in identification with a great purpose, and there is release from tension in throwing oneself into a task worth doing.

All the rest of his life, Peter must have had an understanding of human weakness and a great sympathy for failure and error. If so, his greatness grew out of his worst defeat and became his greatest asset. The stone, which Peter by his own act had placed at the tomb of his hopes and desires, must have seemed to him completely and forever fixed there, and without Jesus' compassionate understanding and God's help it would have been. But the tomb which could not hold Jesus is also powerless to suppress the aspirations of our better natures and the determination to arise and try again.

One snowy night after Christmas our son, who was then in George Washington University, was going to a dinner party over in Arlington, and we were letting him take the car. He was to pick up several others at the university who were also invited and bring them back there afterwards. I was sure it would be late, and I was not at all easy in my mind, so as he got ready I warned him to be exceptionally careful. He was inclined to dismiss my remarks airily. "You know me, Mom."

I said firmly, "Yes, indeed I do, Son, which is exactly why I'm saying all this. If you were to have any trouble in the night— a skid, or a flat tire, maybe—I suppose the first person you would think of calling would be your father."

He said, "Yes, I guess I would, at that."

We both looked at the head of the house who was sitting in his armchair with the newspaper in his lap. His eyes were twinkling. He said, "If you were to get me out of bed at 3:00 A.M. and say, 'Daddy, I'm in trouble. Can you come and help me?' I'd say, 'Who did you say this is?' You'd say, 'It's Steele Hays. Your son.' I'd say, 'I never knew you. Depart from me, you worker of iniquity!' And I'd hang up and get back in bed."

His father might joke, but our son knew he had a resource to turn to, one who wouldn't fail him. A thousand times more solid and secure and faithful than any earthly resource is the Heavenly Father. Fathers and mothers have been known to forsake their children. Friends may turn against us because of a fancied slight. The bank with our life savings may fail. Bombs, they tell us, might fall on Washington and make it a rubble. The only sure thing about this universe is the Heavenly Father and the existence of his home.

I want to tell you the story of a little old lady. Please don't think it is sad. That would be to miss the point. She didn't feel sorry for herself, though she lived at a county farm. She was the last of her family, which had been wealthy. She was not querulous or complaining—she was the same gracious, lovely person she would have been in her own home. She was a bright spot in the life of the young chaplain who ministered to that institution.

But she was old, and her health failed, and finally she knew she wouldn't live in that institution much longer. She was going home. She said to the chaplain, "I've been thinking today of the last service, and I'd like to make a request." (She spoke as if about a farewell tea.)

He said, "Anything."

"It's just a song I'd like sung. 'I'm a Child of the King.'"

The day came, a bleak March day. The little chapel was drab and ugly, and the plain pine box before the chancel depressed the chaplain. They were so unlike her. So unsuitable.

Then a rich contralto voice began to sing, "I'm a Child of the King"!

To the chaplain, at least, the whole scene was transformed, for the words were the truth.

Christians ought to live on Sunrise and greet each day with a song, for we know that in our Father's house are many mansions, and we are expected at home.

Out of the heart are the issues of life.
PROVERBS 4:23

6

Home Is Where the Heart Is
(Mother's and Father's Day)

This is the traditional day for special recognition of mothers. But I have often wished, since I became one, that fathers shared the same day, instead of trailing along a month later like an afterthought or a tail to a kite, and that the emphasis and attention be on life in the family.

It is true that the foundation for the house of life which each must built is laid in infancy and early childhood, and the mother is the chief overseer at this stage. But the father is coarchitect, and he contributes so much—so much of the mother's strength and wisdom is (or should be) drawn from him, and his support of her is so important—that it is hard for her to do the job alone.

God's plan for all little newborn things, plants and animals and human babies, is awe-inspiring. Specific arrangements are made for their protection and warmth and feeding from the moment they are born. Baby birds have a nest waiting for them, the warmth of a mother's feathered breast to cover them, two parents to feed them. Not a single sparrow was ever born without a home waiting for it.

In the plant kingdom the same preparation is made. One example is the baby oak tree. Its first cradle is a little round "fleece"-lined box. When it grows out of that, God teaches it how to reach with little groping fingers down into Mother Earth, for its food is there. It needs sunshine, too, and God provides that. It gets thirsty, so he sends it water to drink.

The little human babies come into the best nests of all. They, too, have two parents, and warmth, protection and food. But there the similarity ends, for being made in the image of God they have both bodies and spirits, and both must be fed in order to grow. God's plan has worked out perfectly for plants and animals, but in the human family it has often broken down, for human parents are the least cooperative. They have sometimes failed their children and they have failed God.

When my sister and I were quite young girls, always either sitting with our noses in books or at the piano playing and singing (except when Mother interrupted us for some trivial thing like a little housework), we were fond of an old ballad entitled, "Home Is Where the Heart Is." It was a love song, which is why we liked it, for our thoughts and dreams centered on love. Not on boys. In the flesh they fell too far short of our ideals. But on Love. I am going to borrow the title but give it a somewhat wider application. I'm using heart in the sense in which the old Hebrew philosopher of Solomon's time used it, "Out of [the heart] are the issues of life" (Prov. 4:23). Or in the words of another, "as [a man] thinketh in his heart, so is he" (Prov. 23:7). And the home has the care and training of the heart in the first, most important years. Home is where the heart is molded and shaped for successful, happy living.

Although he was neither husband nor father, Paul gave advice freely, to husbands, wives, and children. And it was good advice. Many of you would agree that people who do not have children know a good deal about bringing them up. I'm not being sarcastic—or only a little, perhaps. Their emotions are not involved, and they can be objective. Theories often have to be modified, but may serve as ideals. I ascribe whatever success I had to the ideas I had formed and the plans I made before I had any children.

Paul used a significant phrase in a letter to Timothy, when he wrote, "*From a child* thou hast known the holy Scriptures, which are able to make thee wise unto salvation" (2 Tim. 3:15). Timothy was a living example of the influence of a religious home. He will always be a testimonial to the fact that in a home where God is a reality, where the Bible is read, where the parents are people of strong faith, the children will usually grow up to be fine and true.

When Dr. Len Broughton, who was once pastor of the City Temple in London, was asked if he agreed that the source of Britain's strength was its navy, he said no—the source of her strength was the British home.

Home is the bulwark of a free society. We talk too much about the economic foundations of a good society, and not enough about the moral and spiritual foundations. In fact, Dr. Ernest Hocking, a professor at Harvard, said, "It is *only* religion reaching the ultimate solitudes of the soul, for which our pleasing amiabilities are but husks, that can create the unpurchaseable man, and it is only man, unpurchaseable by any society, who can create the sound society."

Children not only need fathers, but I believe men need children. Evidence of this need is seen in the success of an interesting plan adopted by a prison in Salem, Oregon. According to a television program called "Religion in the News," this prison allows and even encourages the inmates to be den fathers for a school of retarded boys. The men volunteer, and there is now a waiting list. (Inmates who fall into certain categories of crimes are excluded.) The boys soon grow to love their "fathers." One man, who has served his sentence, returns to the prison for the den meetings. There is evidently someone in Salem with imagination as well as compassion.

One of the things young people shy away from is discipline, yet unconsciously they crave it, and are insecure and dissatisfied without it. An elderly woman, when asked how she had raised a large family of fine children, said, "I just made sure they got everything that was coming to them, whether it was good or bad."

A black mother, a widow, also had a good system. Her employer has given the following account of it: "Mary used to preside over our kitchen, and I would often hear her commands to her children, 'Stop that shufflin' when you walk,' she would say. 'Pick up your feet and lift up your head like your Pa always done.' When they started to school she urged them to make their time count, so they might 'grow up to amount to something like your Pa did.' And when the girls began to have beaux, they were cautioned to remember their Pa, and not 'come traipsin' in at daylight with some no-count loafer.'

"After years of this, I finally asked Mary what Pa did in this life. Mary laughed scornfully. 'That man never worked nothin' but his jaws! But when he up and left me, back in Atlanta, I made up my mind he wasn't goin' to skip out free. He was goin' to help me raise these young uns somehow! And he did.'"

Sitting with my husband and our Irish host in a small Scotch Presbyterian church in Belfast one Sunday, I heard the minister tell a little story to the children. It was about the grease band that farmers put around their apple trees. In the fall a little insect climbs up the apple tree looking for a place to spend the winter. It finds a small crevice, wraps itself up, and goes to sleep. When the sun warms it in the spring, it wakes up and comes out. Then it begins looking around for a place to lay its egg. It sees the soft heart of an apple blossom, and there deposits the egg, and with a little dab of glue fixes it firmly to the stamen. When the blossom falls off and the little apple begins to swell and grow, the egg is in the center of it. After a while the egg hatches. The codling moth is born. And it finds itself surrounded by delicious food. The apple becomes its pantry as well as its home. On the outside the fruit is perfect, but it is disappointing when cut, for the heart has been ruined by the codling moth.

And so farmers put a grease band around the trees to protect the fruit before it is even formed. Spraying would be useless. The farmers' only defense is to keep the insects from crawling up the trunk.

The children whose parents put a protective band of discipline and ideals around the heart to keep the codling moth of sin— selfishness and other character flaws—from getting a start are the fortunate ones.

Life is easier for those who have been used to discipline, and have made the transition easily from parents' discipline to self-discipline.

A friend told me of the sad case of a young man who had never known restraint. As a premedical student in college, he went in for football and fraternity activities with the attendant social affairs. He wouldn't buckle down to the work required by the course. Exams, of course, were problems until he discovered a technique for carrying facts into the classroom in places other than in his head. He fooled the professors, but it doesn't take genius to do that, merely a certain crafty skill. They were not the ones who suffered because he was cheating his way through. At medical school he was even more clever at cheating, due to several years of practice. In addition, he found a boy whom he could hire to write his term papers. Life was so easy and pleasant that he thought the "grinds" and the "bookworms" were stupid!

But payday came. Life has a way of not cooperating with pretenders, and his patients didn't cooperate either. They died. A farmer who was run over by a truck was one of his first challenges. Then he was called in when a woman developed pneumonia in childbirth. There were others. He had come to the place where he had to deliver the goods—and he had nothing to deliver. That midnight hour when every soul has to unmask struck for him.

"Life," it has been said, "is a just employer. Whatever you ask, Life gladly pays." How tragic it is to find out too late that one has asked only for the most worthless and tawdry things.

It is sad when parents are not disciplined, for no one can guide another who has no complete mastery over himself. A young woman who was once in my missionary circle, the mother of several boys, told something funny about one of them as we were enjoying our tea after the meeting: "Tommy said a ridiculous thing to me yesterday. He said, 'Mother, I wish Daddy was a different kind of man.' I said, 'Why, what kind would you like him to be?' And he said, 'More of the beachcomber type, I guess.' "

We all laughed, but the ones who knew this family best laughed loudest. One of them said, "And that's just what his dad would like to be, isn't it?"

And Tommy's mother said, "Yes. Exactly."

Evidently Tommy was a small chip off the older block. But Tom Senior, who would have loved lying around on beaches in slacks and sport shirts, had to fit a pattern in a civilized society. He had taken on the responsibilities of husband and father, and he had had to discipline himself.

A young man came up for trial in a criminal court. The judge, moved by his youth and attractiveness, asked his name.

"Ohendorfer."

"Where is your home?"

"Chattanooga."

"There is a book in my library called *Equity* written by a man named Ohendorfer. Is he a relation of yours, by any chance?"

"He is my father."

The judge said, "All lawyers know and respect that book."

The boy said bitterly, "My father spent his life writing that book. He never paid much attention to his children."

Another safeguard parents owe their children is ideals, which help to protect the heart against the codling moth.

When former Congressman Porter Hardy of Virginia was given the Brotherhood Award by the National Conference of Christians and Jews, he gave the credit to his father. "He was a Circuit Rider," Mr. Hardy said, "and he used to take me with him. I thought he was the greatest man on earth. He never met a man whom he didn't think of as his brother. I used to ride in his small horse-drawn cart, sitting on a box between his knees, and he preached me many a sermon as we covered the miles. Consequently, I never had any trouble understanding the fatherhood of God and the brotherhood of man."

I well remember the way my mother taught me an important lesson. I was playing dolls with my friend Mary in the shade of our house. It was a hot morning, but cool there, and we were counting on several happy hours. But Mary's mother called her to go on an errand to an old lady's house. Mary came back and asked me to go with her. I didn't want to. I considered it would be a very unrewarding trip—I had been there before. Also, it would be hot and dusty.

Mary said, "I'll give you my doll combs if you will." She knew I had long envied her the box of doll combs. They were white Celluloid, utterly impractical, but fascinating. There were two side combs, a straight comb, and—crowning touch—a round pompadour comb. Mary's offer put a different light on the matter, and I said I would go. Just then my mother called me in. She had heard this business deal, and she said, "Marion, you are forming your character right now. Do you want to be the kind of woman who has to be paid to do a kind deed? If you don't, you must begin now."

That was all. She let me go back and decide. But I knew I

couldn't enjoy the combs now, even if I took them, and I would disappoint my mother.

So I took the hot walk in the sun and didn't get the combs, either. It was painful at the moment, but that very pain helped me to remember the incident. It has come to my mind many times and has had an influence on my life.

When I think of home and family, I cannot help but think of a poem I heard years ago. The name of the author, if ever I knew it, has long since been forgotten.

> I know three things must ever be
> To keep our Nation strong and free.
> One is a hearthstone bright and clear,
> With busy, happy loved ones near.
> One is ready heart and hand
> To keep and serve and love the land.
> One is a worn and beaten way
> To where the people go to pray.
> If all of these are kept alive,
> People and Nation will survive.
> God keep them always, everywhere—
> The home, the flag, the place of prayer.

It is a comely fashion to be glad—
Joy is the grace we say to God.
DOMINIUM

7

Oil, Wine and Weddings
(June: Month of Brides)

June has often been regarded as the brides' month, perhaps because it is also the month of roses, and the two make a beautiful combination, especially if moonlight is added.

Among all peoples, I suppose, the most joyous rite is the wedding, and so it is satisfying to read about the presence of Jesus at a wedding in Cana, a town in Galilee. I think he enjoyed weddings as much as we do. He made them the settings for some of his best stories. There was the big society wedding with ten bridesmaids. (Unfortunately, five of them were very foolish and missed the wedding.) Another was about a man who arranged a marriage feast for his son, only to be bitterly disappointed because the guests refused to come. And one of his most interesting and appealing parallels was the implication that heaven is like a wedding.

How different from the concepts of some preachers of the old school who used to say it would be like an interminable Sunday. Now I like Sunday, but not that well. I like the other six days, too. I once heard a preacher who was evidently not too well-endowed with imagination say it was a place where we would stand around and praise God all day—a wonderful place, he added, defensively, I thought.

Jesus was not responsible for these strange concepts. His picture was quite different. To give us an idea of what heaven is like, he drew on the most joyous event in human experience, a wedding feast. Let's consider the New Testament account of two weddings, one an actual event at which Jesus was a guest; the other, one of his most interesting stories.

The first we might call "Wine at the Wedding," for it is the wine that has gotten the attention, in most people's minds, overshadowing everything else. The story (told by John, in the second chapter) is often classified, and dismissed, simply as the first miracle. The miracle has absorbed us. "Water into wine!" people have exclaimed through the ages; then forgotten the whole thing. Except, perhaps, for those who have felt impelled to change the scripture to suit their notion of what is proper by denying it happened. "It wasn't wine—it was grape juice," they have firmly averred.

But that act of Jesus, miracle or not, be it wine or grape juice, is not the whole of it. It would be revealing and interesting if it did not include a miracle—if in some perfectly natural way Jesus had assisted the host in his embarrassing dilemma. It gains by being removed from the class of statistics, for it gives us an insight into the personality of the young man known as Jesus of Nazareth. A gently-reared young man—brought up by a beautiful and devoted mother, a kindly, just, earthly father, and in constant communication with the Father above—he did not hold himself aloof from any individuals, no matter what their morals or manners.

This family at Cana was not socially prominent. They would not be in the social register. John didn't think their name was important enough to mention. They were just village people. The bridegroom couldn't afford to be wasteful in the matter of wine. He planned economically, just so many firkins, and it wasn't enough. Either more people came than expected (perhaps they brought in-laws or children), or they drank more.

What woman has not known the embarrassment of having something run out? The saying "Family Hold Back" (F.H.B.) was invented for just such occasions. My husband and I were helpless onlookers once when our hostess was caught in a similar situation. She had served us and her other guests glasses of cold raspberry punch. It was a hot day, and the punch tasted delicious. As we sat about talking, still holding our glasses in various stages of depletion, another friend dropped in who was obviously unexpected.

After introductions, he said, "Well, I see I'm just in time to have something good to drink!"

The hostess put her hand over her mouth, a look of sharp anguish on her face. She rolled her eyes appealingly toward her husband, but he looked helplessly back at her. We, the guests, sat in stricken silence. The unexpected one began hastily to say he was just joking, didn't want anything.

"W-would you like a glass of water?" the hostess faltered.

No-no, he didn't care for any water. Wasn't thirsty, really.

Now this was a little neighborhood incident. Unimportant. Soon forgotten. But Jesus in his infinite tenderness would have spared the hostess that embarrassment if he could have. He never laughed when someone was distressed or humiliated. Another's trouble became his own. I believe that characteristic is the one that means most to the world—his sympathy, understanding and compassion. The need, the aching cry, of the world today is for a compassionate Christ to heal the world's wounds. And that is just what he is.

The four Gospels tell us a good deal about what a social person he was. He was not a recluse like John the Baptist. He loved people, and loved being with them. His critics tried to injure him with the taunt that he came "eating and drinking." Why shouldn't he—*they* ate and drank! Some even had the temerity to question him to his face. "John's disciples fast. What's the matter with your disciples that they do not?" When we read the Gospels with this idea in mind, we can see that he was a popular and welcome guest wherever he went. There was no gathering at which he was tongue-tied or ill at ease. Psychologists would say he was a perfectly adjusted individual, for he was always equal to the situation. I think the reason was that he thought of others instead of himself, and that is the best plan anyone can follow for social ease.

Algernon Charles Swinburne in "Hymn to Prosperpine" wrote the grim and bitter line, "Thou hast conquered, O pale Galilean; the world has grown grey from Thy breath." There could never be a greater misconception about the personality of Jesus! His mistaken followers have all too often tried to make the world gray and gloomy in the name of religion, but not Jesus. He came to increase our joys, to make life richer and more abundant, and he began at the wedding feast in Cana.

"Then shall the kingdom of heaven be likened unto ten virgins, which took their lamps, and went forth to meet the bridegroom" (Matt. 25:1).

We know, of course, that Jesus was not giving a lesson on social behavior—how to act when invited to a wedding, what to do if you're a bridesmaid, how to avoid making a faux pas. His stories always had more to them than the obvious surface meaning. Here, he was talking about life in all its grim reality and the necessity of preparedness, not only for death, but for life itself.

In his book *The Way West*, A. B. Guthrie wrote about a wagon train that left Independence, Missouri, in 1845 bound for Oregon. He described the measures taken by those in charge to protect the venture against the easygoing, shiftless irresponsibles who are found in every group. Each man or family had to meet certain conditions. They must take so many pounds of all essentials for each member of the family—meat, flour, meal, bacon, etc. Nobody could go without these things in the proper amounts because if they took along people whose insufficient stores would inevitably give out, it could make the difference between success or failure of the expedition—maybe even life and death. It would deprive others of what they did not have to spare. Selfish? Of course not; just a matter of cool judgment versus irresponsibility.

It's too bad someone wasn't in a position to advise all the bridesmaids to take extra oil, as in the case of the wagon train. But that, too, is a reflection of life. We can't always depend on someone else's giving us the right advice, or any advice at all, and when they do we may not take it. Young people who need it most are the least receptive, but at any age unsolicited advice is not always welcome.

When as a bride I went to live in my husband's hometown, I was introduced to his family's friends and acquaintances, and that was the whole town. Gradually I learned to put names and faces together, and finally to know their individual character- istics. I learned that Mrs. Johnnie Doe was invariably late to everything. She had never trained herself to go by the clock. Many a committee meeting or program at church had to wait on her convenience. When Lucy May Jackson married, she had a church wedding which she wanted to make the last gasp, as far as etiquette went, so she ordained that after her mother was seated the church doors should be locked. This was done. Mrs. Doe, as usual, arrived late and couldn't get in. Some people living across from the church, who were not invited but had window seats for all the coming and going, saw, were amused, and reported. And the word got around town that for once Mrs. Doe had inconvenienced no one but herself!

One of the harsh facts of life is that time waits on no man. Many things have been written on this theme—that life has its deadlines. One of the most familiar is the verse from *The Rubaiyat of Omar Khayyam* translated by Edward Fitzgerald:

> The moving finger writes; and having writ,
> Moves on: nor all your Piety nor Wit
>   Shall lure it back to cancel half a Line,
> Nor all your Tears wash out a Word of it.

One of the saddest little poems in all literature, to me, is in *The Idylls of the King* and was inspired by this parable. Maybe you haven't read it recently, as very few people read Tennyson now. When Guinevere's guilt had become known to Arthur (everyone else knew it already), she fled to a nunnery, in fear for herself and in remorse for the fact that her sin had corrupted the Round Table, and had brought crashing down in ruins Arthur's dreams for a united Kingdom and a circle of Knights who would set an example of nobility and purity for the realm.

But though Guinevere now saw her selfish sin in all its glaring ugliness and longed to expiate it, there was nothing she could do. It was too late; the damage had been done. All her tears could not wipe out a word of it.

A little novice, sent by the nuns to wait upon her in her cell, not knowing the cause of her sadness, sang this song to her:

> "Late, late, so late! and dark the night and chill!
> Late, late, so late! but we can enter still.
> Too late, too late! ye cannot enter now.
>
> "No light had we: for that we do repent;
> And learning this, the bridegroom will relent.
> Too late, too late! ye cannot enter now.
>
> "No light: so late! and dark and chill the night!
> O let us in, that we may find the light!
> Too late, too late! ye cannot enter now.
>
> "Have we not heard the bridegroom is so sweet?
> O let us in, tho' late, to kiss his feet!
> No, no, too late! ye cannot enter now."

Another of the grim facts embodied in this story is that even repentance can come too late—not for the sinner, but to avert the consequences. An example in fact is the case of a boy who had an excellent mind but no sense of responsibility to himself or his parents. He was able to get his lessons quickly and had spare time to play tricks and distract others. In college he didn't improve. He even flunked some courses, but always knew he could easily catch up and get by when he put his mind on it.

However, the thing happened that he did not anticipate— he failed to graduate. He had gone to the brink once too often. This disaster woke him up at last. He was ashamed to go home and face his parents, but he had to take his medicine. He said, "Dad, I've been a fool. I've got to go back next year."

But the father said, "Son, you can't go back next year. The money your mother and I saved for your education is gone. I'm retired now, and we can just get by. You'll have to go to work without your diploma."

The father was sorry for his poor foolish son. There was nothing harsh in his words or manner. In fact, like God, he had been patient far beyond the boy's deserts. The boy's repentance was sincere and deep, but it came too late.

Jesus was not responsible for the grim realities of life. He simply understood them, and he did all he could to prepare and warn his hearers. In this story he is telling us that each one has to live her own life, and on her own oil. Is this philosophy incompatible with the Christian doctrine of the Golden Rule? Or the age-old Hebrew law that one is his brother's keeper? No, for there are ways in which that doctrine does not apply. There are some things we can and should share; others we can't.

One thing that can't be shared or borrowed is skill. The price is high—constant practice and self-discipline—and no one can pay it for another. Another thing that can't be borrowed is wisdom. We can learn from others' experiences and in this way gain some wisdom; but each of us has to do his own growing, mentally as well as physically.

I heard a minister tell sorrowfully about his experiences in two homes which he visited because they were not enlisted in any church, and he had been told the wife and mother in each case was a Baptist. At the first place, the son, a popular football star, was just leaving, and said his parents were out. The minister and the boy talked on the sidewalk, and the latter agreed to come to the church services.

"Would your father come with you?"

"No." He was silent a few minutes, while the minister waited. Then, with a wistful expression, he added, "I wish mother had been faithful to her religion. If she had, I believe Dad would be in the church today."

He paid another visit to a family where all were at home, though the father, who was working in his garage, didn't care to come in. One of the daughters dashed in, said hello and good-by, and ran out to the car of her boyfriend, who was honking impatiently. The second daughter came in wearing a costume so brief the minister thought at first she hadn't finished dressing. The mother explained that she was a model and was going to have her picture made at an ice rink.

"We are so proud of her," the mother said. "She is such a good skater we think she may get to be a professional. And we're proud of our other daughter, too—she has this friend who has a fine job, and a car, and it looks like it might be serious."

"Do they go to church?" the minister asked.

"No, but you see they are just so busy with all their activities they just don't have the time."

The mother was the only one who called herself a Christian, but her letter was in a church in a city they had left six years ago.

(This story was told by Dr. James Eaves, pastor of the First Baptist Church in Albuquerque, New Mexico.)

The two mothers had, each, a tiny lamp, a tiny bit of religion. What will they do when the storms of life come? What will they draw on for spiritual strength? The mothers won't have enough extra oil themselves. They will have nothing to share.

This story may be applied to churches as well as to individuals. They, too, must be on the job. They can waste precious time in many ways. An old lady in the Orient who was nearly blind went to a medical missionary. After an examination he said, "I fear I cannot help you. You have come too late. Why didn't you come sooner?"

She answered, "Why, I have been here all the time. It is you who are late."

This story rings an alarm bell for all who would enter the kingdom of heaven. The sick, the sinful, the sorrowful of the world—"the least of these, my brethren"—are our responsibility and our legacy from Jesus. "And they that were ready went in with him to the marriage. And the door was shut."

8

Sunday Dinner
With a Pharisee
(Summer Traditions)

If honest confession really is good for the soul, then I may effect some slight improvement in mine by admitting that when I think of summer Sundays in my childhood, I think first of fried chicken and hot biscuits, watermelon and homemade peach ice cream.

On the heels of that thought comes church, and what seemed then a very long, dull sermon. Having had very good health, I never missed a Sunday occupying with my mother and sister half of the third pew on the preacher's right hand.

Next, I think of a special kind of conviviality, for it was an old custom, at least in the South, to take someone home for Sunday dinner. And so I have included in this calendar of Special Days the Sabbath day when Jesus was a dinner guest at the home of a wealthy and important Pharisee. As there was no mention of the disciples, I imagine the hospitality of the Pharisee did not exend to them, and Jesus was alone. But he was never lonely, never awkward, never at a loss. Though not born with a silver spoon in his mouth, or used to luxuries, he had such a perceptive sense of real values that he was not overawed by worldly success, nor did he for any other reason stand in awe of his fellow human beings. Bible scholars tell us he was a popular dinner guest, which was due, I think, to a radiance of personality and brilliance as a conversationalist. He was full of stories, and people are always entertained by anecdotes and personal experiences. No party ever got dull, no group got bored, no individual ever dozed, when Jesus was there.

On this occasion he was not among friends. He must have told the disciples afterwards that he knew from the beginning that the Pharisees were watching him. For what reason except that they wanted to get something on him? They hoped he would make a faux pas, or worse—something to tell on him, to ridicule him about. "A rustic Rabbi from Nazareth—you should have seen him, and heard him butcher the language! And his table manners! It was a scream."

But things did not work out according to their plan. Nothing like that happened. A man there who was not identified, a guest or a spectator, had dropsy. Jesus saw him; knew he could heal the man. He looked at the host and his friends. All were Pharisees, some were lawyers. All knew the orthodox and accepted interpretation of the so-called Mosaic Law—which would probably have been unrecognizable to Moses.

Jesus looked around at these men and asked, "Is it lawful to heal on the Sabbath?"

They didn't answer. Their faces closed, they looked back at him silently. There was no one with the understanding and compassion to say, "Well, it *should* be lawful. Do what you can for this poor fellow."

Perhaps they didn't quite dare to say no, for Jesus' skill at showing up his ill-wishers was already known. So they said nothing. But that didn't save them. He asked them another question which they found too embarrassing to answer: "Which of you, if it becomes necessary to save his ox or ass on the Sabbath, refrains?"

Not one said, "*I* refrain." They couldn't. Property was something else! So "they held their peace. And he took him, and healed him, and let him go" (Luke 14:4).

Military men have said the best defense is offense. So while they were at dinner, Jesus attacked. Observing their unseemly and undignified struggle to get the best places for themselves, he said, "When you are invited to a wedding, don't pick out the most important place and go and set yourself down in it. Someone more important than you, for whom the host intended that seat, may arrive, and you may be embarrassed by having to vacate that place and to find yourself a humbler one. Instead of putting yourself forward unbecomingly, take an inconspicuous place. Then you may have the pleasure of hearing your host say, 'Friend, I have a better place for you. Pray, come up higher.' " Then lest anyone fail to get the message, he summed up succinctly, "He that exalts himself shall be abased, and he that humbles himself shall be exalted."

Then, turning directly to the man who had hoped to embarrass him, Jesus said, "Speaking of dinner parties, when you give one don't always invite just friends, your favorite relatives and your rich neighbors—just those you exchange courtesies with, those who will put you on their list and will be sure to invite you to their next party, so that you will receive full benefit from your invitation. Sometimes, give a feast just for the poor, the handicapped, the unfortunate, out of the kindness of your heart, expecting nothing in return. But you will receive something—a blessing from your heavenly Father. He will take care of the recompense."

I wonder what they thought of that! No one commented. Then one of the guests made a pious remark, "Blessed is he that shall eat bread in the Kingdom of God" (Luke 14:15). Well, of course! No one would deny that. But it was a dead-end remark; one of those that puts a period to a subject. It was probably characteristic of Pharisees to utter such pious ejaculations which made them sound holy—to the type who never questions advertisements. There was a certain smug self-congratulation implicit in it; it was saturated with self-righteousness. I think it probable Jesus was answering that smugness, that self-righteousness, when he then told a story about a man who planned an elegant social affair, a great supper, to which he invited a great many guests.

When the night came, he sent his servant to announce to the guests that all was in readiness. And what happened? They had changed their minds. They didn't care to come! The excuses they gave sound very silly, and I suspect Jesus made them so on purpose. One had bought a piece of land and wanted to go see it. Another had bought five yoke of oxen and wanted to try them out. Another said his recent marriage would keep him away. These responses make me think of the farmer who had a shiftless neighbor who was always borrowing. One day he sent over for the farmer's axe. Fed up, the farmer refused; he said he intended to shave that night, and needed it. His wife, who heard, exclaimed, "John! What a silly excuse!" He answered, "One excuse is as good as another if you don't want to do a thing."

The trivial excuses in Jesus' story were just such an affront to the man who had cared enough to make wonderful preparations, and he was angry. He said to his servants, "Go out on the streets and get some hungry and needy people, no matter who, or how they're dressed. Get anyone who will come. Urge them! Not one of those who were first invited shall taste of my supper!"

There the story ends, as far as Luke knew. Did they get the point: that even they, with their complacent assumption that as children of Abraham they would be chief guests at God's table in the new Jerusalem, might find themselves excluded, and that a lot of Gentile and Jewish nobodies would enjoy the feast?

A pretty lively affair, that dinner with the Pharisees! If they wanted something to gossip about, Jesus gave it to them.

Humility has been called the cardinal Christian virtue. I can accept that without feeling it contradicts Paul's statement about the greatness of love in 1 Corinthians 13:13. Rather, it shows the other side of the coin: love is the ideal relationship with others, humility the ideal attitude toward self.

Lord Pakenham, writing in *The Spectator,* made this comment: "I have often thought, I hope not heretically, that humility even more than charity is the distinguishing mark of the Christian. Charity, in the sense of benevolence, may spring from many sources. Humility is in my experience almost inseparable from a Christian conception of the relationship between God and man. For by humility I do not mean a neurotic self-contempt or self-distrust, though there are forms of Christian as of non-Christian neurosis. The Christian realizes on the one hand that he is worthless apart from God; but, on the other, that as a child of God he is infinitely precious and dear to his Father."

The late Dorothy Parker, who was noted for her barbed wit, when told that a certain lady was "awfully kind to her inferiors," asked pointedly, "Where does she find them?" People who are convinced of their own superiority lay themselves open to such snubs.

Group pride is only slightly less nauseating. People can take a modest pride in the accomplishments of their state, political party, denomination or ancestors, but when it becomes an overweening and immodest pride it is an offense to others, a disfavor to the group, and a flaw marring the beauty of the proud one's personality.

There is such a thing as false humility, which is almost as bad as too much self-esteem, for the person who cultivates it in himself invariably makes a virtue of it, and uses it as an alibi for indolence and lack of will. Jesus never felt humble in that way toward his fellow-men. It's the inclusion of God in the equation that gives us a true concept of our own worth, that makes us sensible of the truth that no human yardstick is fit to be used as a scale of measurement. If God occupies his rightful place in our lives, no Christian can be other than sincerely and forever humble. As for our fellows, we are equals, brothers and sisters, children of one Father, and there is no need to feel ourselves basically inferior to anyone.

I think the reason Jesus made so little impression on the Pharisees and won so few of them to his cause was their self-righteousness. They were so wrapped and insulated in it that he couldn't get to them, though he tried with needle-sharp words to pierce it. Yet in their early days, they may have been the ones who exhibited the sincerest piety. But as the years passed they became powerful, respected, rich—and lost their humility. The rift between Pharisees and God grew and widened, and they became pompous and self-important. Finally, they lost all sense of proportion: they were great, the Law was all-important, and God was only a name.

This is not a danger that died with the Pharisees. It is ever present. It mysteriously increases with economic security, for the tendency grows to confuse the world's approval with God's and to substitute dependence on riches for dependence on God.

At the end of the morning service a minister found in his pocket a piece of paper on which was written, "Please pray for a young man who is growing rich very fast." The young man, who apparently didn't want to identify himself, knew that he was in danger and gave a silent cry for help.

Two chaplains, one of whom wore a clerical collar, met on an ocean voyage and became friends. The one whose dress proclaimed his vocation made a point of going all over the ship every single day, never missing a deck or a lounge. The other, thinking he might be searching for someone, finally asked if that were the reason. "Oh, no," was the answer. "I think it does people good merely to see a man of God."

That is a very dangerous idea. The famous Scottish preacher, Alexander Maclaren, said, "When a man suspects he is good, he begins to be bad."

Paul warned us, "[Love] vaunteth not itself, is not puffed up" (1 Cor. 13:4).

And Jesus taught us that we were to make no parade of our virtue. "Let not thy left hand know what thy right hand doeth: That thine alms may be in secret: and thy Father, which seeth in secret himself shall reward thee openly" (Matt. 6:3–4).

Luke records another social affair (Luke 7:36–50) at which Jesus, though an invited guest, was slighted by the host. This gentleman, too, a man named Simon, was a Pharisee, and a resident of Nain, where Jesus was teaching and healing, and his intention was not to honor the young visitor from Nazareth, but to humiliate him.

Again, the disciples were not mentioned, but there were evidently other guests, because the crowd of spectators, who habitually gathered outside an important man's house to watch the arrival of guests, was assembled there.

Also present in the crowd was a woman. She was uninvited. In fact, Simon would not have allowed even the hem of his garment to touch her, for she did not have a good reputation; but somehow she got past the servants. She had come with a purpose—to show her reverence for the young rabbi whose acts and words had reached her heart.

Simon received Jesus in a way that disgraced himself and violated the laws of hospitality. He did not give his guest the customary kiss of greeting, indicating by this omission that he regarded Jesus as an inferior. He sent for no water to bathe his feet nor oil for his head. These courtesies were as elementary as taking a guest's hat and coat and offering him a comfortable seat. Simon's actions were calculatedly offensive.

Then the woman slipped in, carrying a beautiful white box made of alabaster. Her purpose was simply to anoint his feet with soothing, sweet-smelling ointment. She didn't expect to find them dusty! But she saw at once what had happened. I think it was the combination of Simon's neglect and her own consciousness of sin that made her break down. Her tears dripped on his feet, so they were bathed after all, and having no towel she dried them with her long hair. Her tears were the sincere expression of a devoted heart and a remorseful spirit. They cost her more than the ointment, however expensive, and meant more to Jesus.

Simon was disgusted with this vulgar display of emotion, and angered by honor to a guest whom he had not honored. He condemned Jesus for letting a sinful woman touch him. Simon probably had drawn his robe tightly lest he be contaminated, and his face revealed his thoughts for all to see. Jesus read them easily.

"Simon," he said, "I have somewhat to say to you."

"Master, say on," said Simon, with either pretended courtesy or open disdain.

"There was a certain creditor who had two debtors. One owed five hundred pence, and the other fifty. And when they couldn't pay, he forgave both. Which would you say loved him most?"

"Well, I suppose the one to whom he forgave most."

"Right. You see this woman, Simon? You call her a sinner. She was a sinner, true; but she has repented and turned from her sinful life, and God's forgiveness can wipe her sin out. But you, Simon—" And he turned the figurative mirror around so that Simon and his guests could see what Jesus saw: a cold, sneering, arrogant, self-righteous man, a man who had kept the letter of the Law but violated the spirit. Jesus' voice gently but relentlessly fell on Simon's shrinking ears as he listed the insults to an invited guest, the failures of courtesy which did not hurt Jesus but revealed the lack of gentility in Simon.

Then to the woman: "She has loved much. Go in peace." Her sins forgiven, a new life open before her. How happy she must have been that night!

But I don't envy Simon. He had seen himself, an unpleasant experience.

At a certain college they still remember the time when the English professor gave his class a test composed of only two questions. When he wrote the first one on the blackboard, the pupils nearly whistled with delight. It was, "Which of the books you have read so far has interested you least?"

Then he wrote the second, "To what defect in yourself do you attribute this lack of interest?"

That slowed them down. To direct our thoughts inward in an honest effort to see our own weaknesses is good for us. Do you ever ask, "What is wrong with me that I don't like her? That I can't work with him? That I don't appreciate or enjoy certain things?" Our first reaction is that something is wrong—with them.

In all superficial aspects, Simon and the woman present a striking contrast, but they had one thing in common—both were sinners, the woman outside the established religion, Simon within it. He represents a group whose members are legion—the respectable sinners. A writer in the *Christian Herald* said, "The great sins that blight the world are committed by respectable people." Their sins are usually sins of omission—failure of fellowship, failure of love. Simon was guilty of both. Fellowship with Jesus would have led him to develop love for his fellow-man. In Paul's words, the love of Christ constrains us to love our brothers (2 Cor. 5:14).

This story is more evidence that respectable sinners are usually in the economically favored group. It's easy to see why: they are insulated against the seamy side of life, protected against temptation to violence. They have never been hungry enough to steal a loaf of bread, to do something desperate to keep a roof overhead.

Some years ago, the wife of the then President of the United States said publicly, "I made several fruitless attempts to interest the wives of Cabinet members in the need for better housing conditions in Washington."

Their husbands were in powerful positions. They might have had great influence if they had seen the need, had their compassion stirred, been willing to befriend some of those in other walks of life.

Jesus used some of the worst words he knew to describe respectable sinners—whited sepulchers and hypocrites. That means they wore masks. They might be beautifully made-up masks, perfumed, permanented with all the treatment. But the façade is no more real than the beautiful madonnas and saints and angels Michelangelo painted were real, for he got his models from the gutters and alleys of Rome.

Jesus called them blind guides or false guideposts. I remember the days when they were building the network of highways over the United States. Roads weren't well-marked, and we had to grope our way through new territory sometimes. I heard Dr. Clovis Chappell tell about a car trip with his wife in New England when he spent a whole day making a huge circle. Besides the loss of a day, it had another unfortunate result because they stopped to get directions at an antique shop, and that stop "inspired in my wife a passion for antiques which has bewildered and terrified me ever since."

It is unusual to find any flaw in road signs today, and what a convenience that is. However, just last summer we were put to some trouble because a road we were looking for wasn't marked. We were very indignant—we had lost fifteen minutes!

The respectable sinners whom Jesus called "false guideposts" were misleading others on the road of life. They were saying, "Respectability and economic security are the way to eternal life." Less favored people today may also follow the "false guideposts." Looking at their substantial homes, automobiles, and fur coats, they think, "If I could just have those things, I'd have no problems. I'd be perfectly happy."

But that is false philosophy. It is not the way to eternal life nor to happiness here.

I heard on the radio that a man in California stole a street-sweeping machine which was standing idle. But he didn't know how to operate it, and instead of picking up trash as he drove it away, it laid it down. So when the theft was reported, all the police had to do was to follow the trail of rubbish.

The trail of rubbish the materialist lays down will lead to the city dump of life; and when some discover where they are, it may be too late to get back on the right road.

I think some of the most cynical words about life were uttered by Macbeth when he said:

Tomorrow and tomorrow and tomorrow
Creeps in this petty pace from day to day
To the last syllable of recorded time,
And all our yesterdays have lighted fools
The way to dusty death.

He had reason to be gloomy; he had messed up his life and was going to encounter dusty death in the near future. But his words are not true, for they imply that "all our yesterdays" add up to futility and waste and false directives. If they had, this old world might have piled up on the dust heap long ago.

But there have been innumerable men and women whose yesterdays and todays have been true guides. Keeping unswervingly to the straight and narrow road pointed out by Jesus, they have been a light to keep other wayfarers, though fools, from losing their way.

Breathes there the man, with soul so dead,
Who never to himself hath said,
*   This is my own, my native land!*
Whose heart hath ne'er within him burn'd
As home his footsteps he hath turn'd,
*   From wandering on a foreign strand?*

SIR WALTER SCOTT

9

The American Dream
(Independence Day)

We are not concerned with dead souls but with live Americans who love their country, whose hearts do burn with pride, who thrill to the sight of Old Glory waving in the breeze, and who would protest to their last breath that they would never fail nor forsake her.

But there are ways in which the most self-convinced patriot may fail his country without realizing it, for true patriotism involves much more than a public display of symbols such as wearing a flag lapel pin, repeating the oath of allegiance, and knowing more than one verse of *The Star-Spangled Banner.*

In the Great War, a man who had some grievances, real or fancied, against the government was drafted and went to France. But there, he defected to the enemy. He surrendered to some German soldiers, who took him in. The German officers had some suspicions that his capitulation was not genuine, that in fact he might be a spy, and told him to prove his sincerity by trampling on an American flag they had captured.

His face flushed, and he said, "But that's Old Glory! I couldn't do that! I couldn't step on Old Glory!"

He could turn against his countrymen. He could let his resentment against a few lead him into betrayal of all the rest, but he couldn't scorn or desecrate the flag. But what did it mean to him? A flag is nothing but a piece of dyed cloth if it doesn't stand for love of country, duty to one's fellow-men, and a feeling of responsibility for promoting the welfare of our citizens and preserving the highest values of our history.

There are other ways of failing our country, of undercutting her strength and power, than by trampling on Old Glory. One is by putting our state or section first.

A few years ago, at the height of the racial tensions, my husband and I went to South Carolina for some speeches he was going to make at one of the colleges. The event had been publicized in the newspapers. The night before his first address, the local head of the Veterans of Foreign Wars called our room at the hotel, got Brooks, and said in an offensive manner, "I want to protest your coming here to speak."

Brooks was staggered. Nothing like that had ever happened to him before. But he pulled himself together and said, "I'm a veteran. I've worn the uniform of my country. I'm a member of the American Legion. Do you question my patriotism?"

"No—no," the man said.

"Then on what basis do you object to my speaking as an American in your state?"

"You come down here to discuss race questions. You're a traitor to the South!"

Brooks exclaimed, "Do you put the South above the United States?" and, incredibly, he answered, "You're damn right I do!"

I remember the inspiring example set by Senator Warren Austin of Vermont when he was named our first ambassador to the United Nations. He said he had three flags on his desk. One was the flag of his little Green Mountain State which he dearly loved. Beside it, was the Stars and Stripes. He said he did not love Vermont any less because he also loved his country. When he added the blue and white standard of the United Nations, it did not take away any of the loyalty and devotion he gave the other two, for such feelings are not exclusive. One of the surest laws of life is that love is not diminished by use; on the contrary, the more we love, the more love we have to give. A few patriots of the quality of Warren Austin are worth thousands of the type of that other who had room in his stunted little heart for only one thing at a time.

Demagogues, both religious and political, have found that an appeal to sectional or class prejudice is a sure-fire way to stir up feeling and to gain a following.

The disease of conformity, which is so contagious it can spread like an epidemic and do as much damage, is increased and spread by those who are the most vociferous in their professions of loyalty, and the most ruthless in condemning others whose love of country is expressed differently. I am thinking of the McCarthy era, one of the saddest in our history, for the American people panicked. They began by being afraid to resist the trend of public opinion; then they allowed their fears to be whipped up, turned on anyone that was accused, and ended by becoming a mob.

A man who owned a clothing store in a Texas city told my husband that during that period of trauma, a friend came into the store and said, "Matt, I'm closing out my account with you. You're a Communist, and I'm not going to trade with you any longer."

"But, Sam, I'm *not* a Communist!"

"You are in my book. You've been supporting a soup kitchen down on Market Place, and that's been shown up to be a Communist outfit."

"Well, I did give them a fifty-dollar check, but that's all, and it was to feed hungry people. That doesn't make me a Communist."

Sam insisted it did and said neither he nor his wife would trade there any more.

Matt said to Brooks, "Maybe some Communists did infiltrate that soup kitchen, which was known to be feeding some strikers— pecan pickers who were getting only three dollars for a week's work. They were striking for four. My friend didn't forgive me, but," he chuckled "I didn't lose his business! He didn't know it, but his wife continued to trade with us—she sneaked in and paid cash."

Which was the better man? The superpatriot? Or the one who showed mercy?

Many a true American had to defend himself against a sick society, when his only fault was in being overly generous in lending his name or influence to an organization which for some reason became suspect. One was the late revered Bishop Oxnam of the United Methodist Church, who had to appear before the Committee on Un-American Activities to defend his loyalty, an indescribable humiliation for an honorable and scholarly man. Silly people asked, "Well, why did he join all those things?" It was a way of asking, "Why would he want to help all those people?" They couldn't understand that because they were perfectly happy doing nothing for anybody—and a whole lot safer.

Dr. Albert Schweitzer, not long before he died, warned us that we are living in the most dangerous period in history because man learned to control elemental forces before he learned to control himself. Most of us allow our pride in our great technological achievements to obscure the fact that in other ways we have not kept pace. We have conquered the air, have been to the moon, and have begun to investigate other planets, but we have not succeeded in mastering our own spirits.

James Thurber, in *Further Fables for Our Time*, described a conference of ostriches who were dejected because they could not fly. One, whose name was Oliver, complained it was unfair that while ostriches are denied the joy of flight, man can even fly sitting down.

Then a wise old ostrich pointed out to Oliver, "Man is flying too fast for a world that is round. Soon he will catch up with himself in a great rear-end collision, and Man will never know that what hit Man from behind was Man."*

We have just come through a very traumatic period. One speaker, in the early part of this decade (the seventies), said we were on the verge of a national nervous breakdown. But we *did* come through—a great testimonial to the soundness of the Ship of State.

In *Pilgrim's Progress,* Mr. Badman asks Christian, "What do you think of the times?"

Christian answered: "They are bad because men are bad. If men would mend, so would the times."

I think men—and women—are mending now. They are trying to do better than they have done—to act more justly, to show more mercy. I lost some of my distress over the bad times when I heard Dr. Harold Phillips say, "Dynamic ages such as this are creative ages. God can do more when the waters are stirred."

It would be wonderful if, as a nation, we could claim to have achieved the goals and realized the ideal which we proudly call the American dream.

What is the American dream? It may mean many things, but if we search for words to express our feelings, we would surely include freedom and justice and peace. It is appropriate and significant that on the Liberty Bell is inscribed a line from Leviticus, "Proclaim liberty throughout all the land and unto all the inhabitants thereof" (Lev. 25:10), for our country was founded on religious ideals.

Yes, liberty from England was achieved. We fought our mother country to secure it. But we were fighting not only for political freedom, but for freedom of religion, of assembly, of speech. There are other important freedoms we do not yet have. "Liberty and *justice for all*" is so stated in one of our great public docu-

---

* James Thurber, *Further Fables for Our Time* (New York: Simon and Schuster, 1956), p. 169.

ments. But we the people have not seen to it that there is justice for all, and we do not have freedom from fear, want, and ignorance.

A true patriot is concerned about the rights of others. Most of us are extremely interested in our own rights, but not equally concerned about our responsibilities, and these include the rights of others. Dr. Billy Graham called this a "national sin" and pointed out that citizenship is both a right and a responsibility. When we shirk the responsibility we begin to lose the rights.

The Women's Christian Temperance Union enlarged its vision and expanded the bounds of its patriotism when it changed its motto from "For God and Home and Native Land" to "For God and Home and Every Land." A similar spirit was expressed by Catherine Lee Bates at a dinner in her honor in New York when the toastmaster said, "Your hymn, 'America the Beautiful,' says everything. It is the last word. Nothing more satisfying can ever be written."

Miss Bates answered, "You are wrong. It doesn't go nearly far enough. It is out of date already. We need a world hymn."

Patriotism which does not stop at the water's edge, but remembers we are just a part of the world which God loves, will make us better Americans.

Once in a seminar of college students my husband mentioned the American dream, and a student asked if he would define it. Slowly and thoughtfully, but with complete spontaneity, he said this:

What is the American dream?
It is the anticipation that sometime we will be able to say—
Here is equality and freedom;
Here is brotherhood and justice.
The dream is of compassion expressing itself in society's concern for those who fall by the way in a competitive system.
It is imagination perfecting the mechanisms of government.
It is sensitivity to the claim of righteousness in human affairs.

It is the hope that triumphs here will strengthen values that are shared with other people around the world.

It is human kindness so penetrating the nation that every man, no matter how incapacitated, will feel that he is wanted.

It is the vision of opened doors of opportunity.

It is insistence upon government *by* as well as *of* and *for* the people.

It is the hope of human dignity made secure.

It is the longing for acknowledgment of the human family's oneness.

It is the vision of a citizenry drawn together in mutual confidence, facing common evils and exalting a common faith in God.

This is my conception of the American dream.

Even in the midst of busy city streets,
an unexpected spot of greenery with the
smell of new-cut grass can evoke green
thoughts, create a summer of the mind,
a holiday of the heart.
CHRISTIAN SCIENCE MONITOR

I am the bread of life: he that cometh to
me shall never hunger; and he that believeth
on me shall never thirst.
JOHN 6:35

10

Summer Reveries
(Vacation Time)

August, in my salad days in a southern town, was the month of idleness, when the grownups sat on their porches in the morning, languidly waving palm leaf fans, and retired to darkened bedrooms after lunch (which was called dinner) until time to again make their appearance on the porch. Those were the days of friendly neighborhood visiting—everyone was visible at the same hours. One point of contact was at the fruit and vegetable wagons which rolled daily along the street, almost in procession. The housewives chatted as they gathered around them to select their peaches, watermelons, roasting ears, and peas and beans still in their pods.

Children enjoyed increased freedom from their share of household tasks because it was recognized that holiday time was flying swiftly by and school bells would soon be recalling them to nine months of regimentation. This escape from routine was one of the delightful aspects of August, triumphing even over the heat. The rich people in our town escaped to resorts in the Ozark Mountains, Eureka Springs and Siloam, Winslow and Mountainburg. The rest of us just escaped into idleness. As we had never been to any of those places, my sister and I did not miss them, and we just enjoyed what we had—plenty of time to do nothing but read and dream.

Andrew Marvell, writing about the lovely gardens of England, called them verdurous spots whose effect on the mind is to annihilate "all that's made, to a green thought in a green shade." How delightfully cool and lazy!

Emily Dickinson expressed her feeling about the pleasure of lassitude in these lines:

> To make a prairie it takes a clover and one bee,
> One clover, and a bee,
> And revery.
> The revery alone will do,
> If bees are few.

And in another mood, perhaps, she wrote this:

> Oh Sacrament of summer days,
> Oh Last Communion in the Haze—
> Permit a child to join.
> Thy sacred emblems to partake—
> Thy consecrated bread to take
> And thine immortal wine!

The combination of summer and food brings me, not too obscurely, I hope, to a picnic which took place on a hill in Galilee.

Did you ever wonder whether Jesus liked picnics? There was certainly an affinity between him and nature. We know he loved the outdoors, the mountains, the sea. Well, at least once (Matthew and Mark say twice), he was the inspiration for a picnic; in fact, he suggested it. There was a big crowd which had followed him out into the country to a lovely mountainside with trees to sit under, rocks to sit on, and outdoor air to sharpen hunger. When mealtime came, Jesus said, "Let's have a picnic."

The disciples, who were often literal-minded wet blankets—like some of us, maybe—said, "Where will we get food?"

Jesus said, "Well, what do we have with us? See if people have brought along lunches."

No, they hadn't known they were going so far away, or would be gone so long. Only one little boy had a lunch, but he turned it over willingly. And Jesus blessed it and divided it. And God magnified it. In his hands it became a great deal, refreshing and giving new strength to many people.

The significance of this story for us, I think, is in its symbolism. It illustrates several of the great concepts of Christianity.

Let's consider Jesus in his relation to those at the picnic.

First, Jesus and the multitude. The crowd forgot the dusty miles, forgot mealtime, forgot tired feet in their eagerness to hear him. But finally, their bodies made demands; they were hungry and thirsty. Many had private worries, sickness at home, money troubles, sins. But whatever else was true, Jesus knew that all were hungry, and he was concerned. He had compassion on the multitude.

The disciples did not. "Send them away," was their advice. "Get rid of them. Let them go to some village and buy themselves something." Their feeling was typical of the time. The general attitude toward people in the mass was one of contempt. J. M. Dawson, long-time pastor of the First Baptist Church in Waco, Texas, has written, "All the splendid intellectualism of Greece existed for the favored few; beneath that glittering edifice of art and letters lay dungeons of slaves. In Rome it was the same. It was an empire of privilege in which the multitude had no part. Jewish society, too, was built on the same pattern." But there was one difference—one based on religious snobbishness, which bred a kind of arrogance even more intolerant and bitter.

But how different Jesus was! To realize how he stood out alone against the customs of the day makes us appreciate him even more. Those people may not all have been of his religious faith, or of any faith at all. There were lots of people in Palestine. He didn't inquire how many were Pharisees, or Jews, even. He wouldn't have cared if they had been Methodists or Baptists! Only one thing mattered: they were hungry.

It has been said that we will never understand this miracle until we can feel the compassion of Jesus. So maybe some of us never will understand. We don't even know how it feels to be hungry. Oh, we've been pleasantly hungry, knowing we can satisfy it as soon as we care to.

We enjoyed a little joke on my mother, once, when I was a girl. One evening as she was rolling out biscuit dough for our supper, she was so hungry she was afraid the usual pan full wasn't going to be enough. She felt that she could eat that many all by herself. When two friends dropped in for a little visit and she asked them to stay for supper, she made up another batch. She kept putting in a little more milk and flour and shortening, and then worried for fear she wouldn't have enough for herself. As it turned out, she had biscuits to give the chickens! Nobody else was as hungry as she was.

To be hungry when you know food is available is wonderful. But to be hungry and to have nothing to satisfy it with is another matter altogether.

By his compassion for the tired, hungry crowd, Jesus revealed how God feels about us. He cares about our human needs. He knows we need food and shelter, and he wants our trust. Anything we need, he will help us obtain. Our trust makes it easier, somehow releases his power.

Martin Luther said the preacher he loved best was one that taught him trust. "I have one preacher that I love better than any other on earth," he wrote. "It is my little tame robin, who preaches to me daily. I put crumbs upon my window sill, especially at night. He hops onto the window sill and takes as much as he needs. From there he always hops to a little tree nearby and lifts his voice to God and sings his carol of praise and gratitude. Then he tucks his little head under his wing and goes fast asleep, leaving tomorrow to look after itself. He is the best preacher that I have on earth."

Second, Jesus and the little boy. I wish I knew his name. He is an example to us, a good example, of an obedient disciple. When Jesus asked him for something, he did not withhold it. He didn't question, "What use is my little bit?" He did not complain, "Why should I be the one to look out for all these people? I don't even know them." He did not delay; "I'll just see what others give first." He gave all he had cheerfully, willingly, and promptly. One more thing he didn't do—try to divide and pass his bread and fish himself. He gave it to Jesus to do it for him.

A modern adaptation of this story, a repetition of the miracle that was the result of unselfish sharing, occurred when a little nine-year-old Chinese boy living in Manila heard his mother and father discussing the sad case of children in China; many were starving. This little boy had fourteen pesos of his own. He was saving it for a bicycle. But he quickly decided that he couldn't enjoy a bicycle after hearing that. So, taking his savings, he went to the nearest bakery and asked for fourteen pesos' worth of bread. He had taken a handcart with him, and this was loaded with the loaves.

He rolled them to the Chinese YMCA and explained to the secretary that they were his gift to the Chinese children back "at home."

As I read this story, I was filled with admiration for the secretary. He was the right man in the right place. He may have been momentarily stumped, but he did not say, "Sonny, we can't send this bread. It would be too stale to eat." He thanked the little boy as courteously as if he had been a man and helped unload the bread. Maybe while he was unloading it the idea came. Maybe he prayed for one. He put people to work phoning

members of the YMCA and YWCA boards and some other
public-spirited people. He asked them to come to the YMCA
that evening for something special. They came. The secretary
told the story, and then auctioned the bread. The people present
gave 1,254 pesos, and it was sent to China. I don't know what
year that was, nor the political condition of China, but the story
is true, so that doesn't matter.

The little boy's contribution was increased by almost 100 percent. Once more the power of God, in people's hearts, brought
about a miracle.

Third, Jesus and the disciples. We see that Jesus turned over
to them the responsibility and the task of passing the food,
for many hands were necessary. He said to them, and to us,
"Give ye them to eat." Without question, complaint, or favorit-
ism, give to all of them with no exceptions.

Great masses of the world's population, some of them Americans, are still hungry. One third of them will go to bed hungry
tonight while we stuff ourselves. We had dinner one evening
with four friends who had just been to a wedding followed by
a reception at one of Washington's big hotels, and they gave
us a description of the lavish buffet supper served to four or
five hundred guests. There was a long line extending well up
the hotel corridor, and the whole time they were moving gradually
toward the ballroom and the receiving line, waiters were busily
serving drinks to them as if afraid they might perish of thirst
before they could get inside. The buffet supper was very unusual
(to say the least) for a wedding: cold meats, hot meats, casseroles,
salads, jellied whole fish, etc. Our friends estimated the cost at
from ten to fifty thousand dollars. I was thankful we hadn't
gotten an invitation which would have called for a costly present
in keeping with the occasion—I wasn't that hungry! One of
our four friends had been trying to get her weight down, and
that buffet bounced her right off her wagon.

There is nothing wicked about that kind of display. I'm not

suggesting it. But it is revealing. It tells a great deal about the values and priorities of a family. And it represents such an appalling waste. Jesus said, "Feed the hungry," not the overstuffed. Yet some church members are more distessed at the thought that some people are on the welfare rolls who don't deserve to be there. Do we deserve to have food to waste?

I believe it was Teddy Roosevelt who said, "Some day it will be considered a crime for some to have too much while others have too little."

I heard Dr. John Peters, the founder of an organization he called World Neighbors, tell about his struggle to get a college education during the depression. There was one two-week period when he had only fifteen cents a day for food. He would buy a coke and two packages of "nibs." It was not enough. When he saw others eating steaks, pork chops, salads, and pies, he hated them. They were not to blame; they didn't know him or that he was hungry. "But," he said, "hunger has its own peculiar logic. And when we show them—the poor, at home and in other countries—through our movies, propaganda, and actions when traveling, how well-off we are, how well-fed, they don't love us. They tighten their belts and hate us a little more."

The logic of hate, which breeds fear and distrust and war, must give way to the logic of love if we would have peace.

Of course, one of the great affirmations of Jesus is that man does not live by bread alone, but also by the words of God. He supplied both, taking care of the human need first, and he expects us to do the same. Some must be fed before they can learn. And some are behind the Iron Curtain and the Bamboo Curtain and must be reached.

There was a baker in Hong Kong during World War II who had the imagination and the ingenuity to do both. Before Hong Kong fell, his bread, packaged in cans, was sold throughout China. A Christian, he knew the importance of both kinds of bread, and so in each can he put a slip of paper with the printed words of John 6:35 in four languages (Chinese, Japanese, Malay and English). Many people wrote to the baker asking who Jesus was and what the words meant.

He would send back a little booklet of the Gospel of John in their own language. Only God knows how many souls may have been fed by that one man.

> "Live and let live!" was the call of the Old—
> The call of the world when the world was cold—
> The call of men when they pulled apart—
> The call of the race with a chill on the heart.
>
> But "live and help live!" is the cry of the New—
> The cry of the world with the Dream shining through—
> The cry of the Brother World rising to birth—
> The cry of the Christ for a Comrade-like earth.
> —Edwin Markham, "Live and Help Live"

And gladly wolde he lerne, and gladly teche.
GEOFFREY CHAUCER

*So teach us to number our days, that we
may apply our hearts unto wisdom.*
PSALMS 90:12

11

Labor Days
(Back to School)

Vacation is over. It's time to go back to work, for, to paraphrase
Shelley, "O, Wind, if August comes, can school days be far
behind?" Not that all of us are going back to the classroom,
but the arrival of September is just a reminder that we are not
and never will be alumni in the school of life, for we have to
keep growing mentally and spiritually as long as we live. We
are never too old or too tired for our spiritual activity to be of
primary importance. In fact, as we get older, we have to be
more alert and persevering lest we sag in our virtues as we do
in our figures.

Jesus made a humorous reference to the uselessness of trying
to change one's physical shape by "taking thought," but he referred only to height, not width. The latter *is* amenable to
thought plus will.

Paul, writing to the Christians at Philippi, urged them to
think as a step in spiritual development. To be sure they understood him, he told them what to think about: the virtues that

95

should be the attributes of a Christian—honesty, truth, justice, purity, loveliness of character (Phil. 4:8). He probably didn't realize how hard thinking is for most of us. To concentrate on one idea for fifteen or twenty minutes is really difficult.

A man in H. G. Wells's "The Croquet Player" says, "I am willing to fall in with anything that promises any good. But if I am to *think*, it is too much." Most of us are not that honest, even with ourselves.

Our thoughts are full of the important (or so it seems) trivia of everyday living. We can sympathize with the maid who heaved such a gusty sigh her mistress asked if something were wrong. "No'm, just life is so daily, ain't it?"

We don't need to make an effort to think on these things, but we do need to make a distinct effort to shut them out, for we tend to become like the things we think about. If we keep our minds filled with small things, we will become small-souled. If Paul had said, "Sit down and think what a good time you had the other day," wouldn't that be easy? But that is just remembering, which is what passes for thinking with many of us most of the time.

An elderly deaf woman (who would probably have maintained that she was a better-than-average Christian because she invoked God a great deal) loved to play bridge. She had fallen into the habit of uttering her thoughts and even her prayers aloud, forgetting others could hear what she couldn't. She was very devout by her own definition which meant that God was always on her side, her silent partner, and she would talk to this partner frequently and audibly. She would mutter, "Oh God, now give me a good hand! . . . I need an ace, Lord; give me an ace. . . . Please, Lord, help me to play this hand right. . . ."

She had the Christian ideal twisted around: instead of being God's steward, he was the steward of *her* possessions; she expected him to serve her! A little straight thinking would have done that woman good.

I recently saw expressed the following imaginative little

thought: "Ideas, light as goose feathers, are all around us if one has eyes sharp enough to see and ears to hear."

Most of us, I think, should listen more than we do. A reputation for talking nonstop is seldom an asset. In 1944 my husband was selected for a special mission for the President and told to suggest a colleague in the Congress to accompany him. He named a congenial friend in the other political party. In a few days the answer came—choose someone else. The first man, they said, talks too much. He never listens to others; therefore, he misses information.

In following Paul's counsel to think about spiritual things, the first step is to be still. When the psalmist wrote, "Be still, and know that I am God," he may have been sharing with us his own experience. If we would have God speak to us, we must be quiet, and then "the peace of God which passes all understanding" can quiet our restless hands and minds. Fifteen minutes spent quietly with God every day would keep people out of sanitariums, I believe. He is waiting to bestow his peace upon any who will just be still and receive the gift of his grace. E. Stanley Jones once wrote, "The streams that turn the machinery of the world take their rise in silent places."

The treatment of religious matters in fiction is often amazingly irritating to me. A notable exception is a conversation between a seventeen-year-old girl and the Vicar in *I Capture the Castle* by Dodie Smith. The girl, Cassandra, tells the story. She was unhappily in love with a young man who was in love with her sister, Rose.

> On the Wednesday of that week of mud and misery I went to see the Vicar. . . . I [had] a feeling that a person as wretched as I was ought to be able to get some . . . help from the Church. Then I told myself that as I never gave the Church a thought when I was feeling happy, I could hardly expect it to do anything for me when I wasn't. You can't get insurance money without paying in premiums.

I found the Vicar starting to plan a sermon . . . "Now this is splendid," he said. "An excuse to stop working—and to light a fire."

. . . After [a little], we got started on religion, which surprised me rather, as the Vicar so seldom mentions it—I mean to our family; naturally, it must come up in his daily life.

"You ought to try it, one of these days," he said. "I believe you'd like it."

I said: "But I have tried it, haven't I? I've been to church. It never seems to take."

He laughed and said he knew I'd exposed myself to infection occasionally. "But catching things depends so much on one's state of health. You should look in on the church if ever you're mentally run down."

. . . "Oh, it wouldn't be fair to rush to church because one was miserable," I said.

"It'd be most unfair not to—you'd be doing religion out of its very best chance."

"You mean 'Man's extremity is God's opportunity'?"

"Exactly. Of course, there are extremities at either end; extreme happiness invites religion almost as much as extreme misery."

I told him I'd never thought of that. . . .

. . ."If any—well, unreligious person needed consolation from religion, I'd advise him or her to sit in an empty church. Sit, not kneel. And listen, not pray. Prayer's a very tricky business."

"Goodness, is it?"

"Well, for inexperienced pray-ers, it sometimes is. You see, they're apt to think of God as a slot-machine. If nothing comes out, they say, 'I knew dashed well it was empty'—when the whole secret of prayer is knowing the machine's full."

"But how can one know?"

"By filling it oneself."

"With faith?"

"With faith. . . . If ever you're feeling very unhappy . . . try sitting in an empty church."

. . . Then we fell silent, both of us staring at the fire. Rain kept falling down the chimney, making little hissing noises. I thought what a good man he is, yet never annoyingly holy. And it struck me for the first time that if such a clever, highly-educated man can believe in religion, it is impudent of an ignorant person like me to feel bored and superior about it. . . .*

We know that the time of communion is not an end in itself, but only the necessary preparation for our Christian service. There is a verse in the Old Testament (Ezek. 2:1) which represents God as saying, "Stand upon thy feet, and I will speak unto thee." He is talking to man.

I think we might interpret that as God's call to the human race to emerge from savagery: "Stand up. I can't communicate with animals. You're a man—destined for companionship with God."

But we can also say it is not only his call to the race, but to each individual soul: "Stand as tall as you can. If others are crawling, encourage them to stand, but on no account get down and descend to crawling yourself." We are so inclined to look around and see what others are doing. If we see many who are self-centered and small-minded, we relax. But they are not the ones to emulate. A writer, Harold Blake Walker, used the phrase, "competing against ourselves." We must ignore those who do not offer us any competition and keep an eye on our own record: "What did I give to life yesterday? I must give more today. Did I fall back yesterday? Today I must go forward." To borrow from Dr. Walker again, "Yesterday's mistakes and failures can teach us wisdom, and yesterday's triumphs can suggest what is possible."

On a trip to New England in our car, as we drove along beautiful New Hampshire roads, winding through woods turning red and gold, we got behind a poky driver. We were fifth in line, and the procession behind us was growing. Brooks said, "That's the reason for the signs you see sometimes, 'Minimum speed forty miles an hour.' A minimum can create a hazard, too."

* Dodie Smith, *I Capture the Castle* (Boston: Little, Brown and Company, 1948), pp. 232–36.

He didn't know he was giving me a point for the Sunday School lesson I was even then working on. A lazy Christian, living at a minimum of effort, giving to life a minimum of love, can create a greater hazard than any traffic problem, for the consequences are so much more important. They send out silent calls to those about them to relax. "No need to be so earnest, so unstinting. Take it easy!"

Many of you will remember when Marie Curie, a scientist who was also a mother and housewife, amazed the world by isolating a new and hitherto unknown element—radium—which proved to be of inestimable benefit to mankind. It was the result of a laborious process. Helped by her husband, Pierre, who was working on scientific projects of his own, she made 487 experiments, trying to separate from pitchblende the element she believed was there. All failed. One day Pierre was so discouraged he exclaimed, "It can't be done! Maybe in a hundred years—never in our lifetime."

But Marie, as tired as her husband, said, "If it takes one hundred years it will be a pity. But I dare not do less than work for it as long as I have life."

What if she had relaxed because other women were not knocking themselves out trying to help humanity? The world would have been the worse off, and so would Marie. She competed against herself, and she achieved greatness. The whole world accords her honor. But her greatest accolade would have been the divine approval, "Well done, good and faithful. . . ."

Someone said, "Religion is a stream where elephants can swim and lambs can wade." A way of saying there is a depth for everyone. It can accommodate the crawlers. But the deeps are for those who greatly love and greatly dare, and for whom religion is a wonderful adventure.

My thoughts are not your thoughts; neither
are your ways my ways, saith the Lord.
ISAIAH 55:8

The heart has its reasons
which reason does not know.
BLAISE PASCAL

12

The Grape Pickers
(Harvest Time)

Jesus was the greatest of all teachers because his message was unparalleled, and his life exemplified it without a flaw.

Paul said that after the prophets, God spoke through his Son (Heb. 1:2), and never has there been such a Voice. It was the Word made flesh, and the Word was Love.

Let us consider *how* he presented his message. The very first time he spoke, in a synagogue in Capernaum, he startled his audience, for unlike the scribes, who did nothing but quote the Law and the prophets, he took responsibility for everything he said. He uttered what he knew to be truth, and he didn't need any other authority for that. No wonder it was said that no other man spoke like this one! Authority is a mark of kingliness, of leadership. It impels obedience.

Shakespeare has a nice comment on this fact in *King Lear* in a brief exchange between the King and the Earl of Kent, who is in disguise (act 1, scene 4).

King: Who wouldst thou serve?
Kent: You.

King: Does thou know me, fellow?
Kent: No, sir; but you have that in your countenance which I would fain call master.
King: What's that?
Kent: Authority.

Jesus' voice was the voice of Truth. In two thousand years he has never been successfully contradicted. Nothing he ever said has become obsolete. His wisdom has never been even approximated in one person. Rather than a supernatural revelation, I prefer to think it was due to his close association with God. As he grew in stature, he grew in wisdom and favor. If we lived as close to God as he did, I think we would be much wiser than we are.

Another thing we notice about Jesus' teaching methods is that places were unimportant to him. He created his own atmosphere. He never had to have a pulpit. Whether he sat in a boat, or under a tree on a hillside, or in a home, he was surrounded by eager listeners. I don't believe anyone ever dozed, or became bored, or left early when they had a chance to hear Jesus. His talks were liberally and delightfully sprinkled with illustrations. Indeed, we owe to them the fact that so much was remembered by his biographers, or passed on to them by those who did remember.

My husband has had abundant evidence that stories linger in the memory long after everything else in a speech has been forgotten. With some slight variation of details, he hears often such remarks as, "I heard you speak only once, years ago, but I still remember a story you told." Two thousand years after he told them, we are still reading and hearing Jesus' stories.

These stories, or parables, were full of human interest, and included a wide range of subjects from kings to thieves, from pearls to yeast. Rich men and great lords frequently appeared in them, but usually represented God. Every story had details of a life they understood—a farmer sowing or reaping, a woman making bread, another losing a precious coin.

Of course, in the crowds that followed Jesus, there were some who didn't understand what he was telling them and complained about it. "I don't get it. What's he talking about? What does he mean?" The disciples didn't always get it, either, you remember, and would ask him afterwards, privately, so as not to expose their own ignorance, "Now explain it to us." And he always did.

Jesus is still criticized by people who don't want to be put to the trouble of applying their own judgment. They say the "weakness" of the Sermon on the Mount is that it leaves too many choices to the individual. It is too indefinite. But isn't that what he intended to do—leave the final choice to the individual? The talks collected and compiled by Matthew which we call the Sermon on the Mount make little mention of personal habits or codes of conduct. It is not a set of rules or "Thou shalt nots." We have the Ten Commandments in common with the Jews, and they are basic to religion and morality. But many people would like to add some other taboos which would be no temptation to them and would make discipleship much easier than cultivating the spirit of Christ.

Some time ago I saw a program on television which was sponsored by Princeton University in which a Catholic priest was questioned by a panel. He had reached a place of distinction in his church because of years spent as a social worker. One panelist asked him, "Did Jesus ever settle any sociological problems?"

He answered, "No, he did not. He did something better. He tried to create an atmosphere and cultivate an attitude of heart and mind in which men could solve their own problems in the right way—the way of love."

And so we must accept the fact that we don't find the answers to our problems in *specifics* set out by Jesus. We find them in principles, abstractions, and affirmations—a course which requires a reaching up, a stretching of mind and heart and soul.

Someone said that abstract ideas are like empty picture frames in which Jesus hung pictures. I'd like for us to look closely at one of those oral pictures which I will call *The Grape Pickers*. It has been more often ignored than admired, for it is a little difficult to understand. On the surface it doesn't seem reasonable. In fact, it makes God, who we know is the householder, sound like an eccentric or at least unconventional. We can't help wondering what a modern efficiency expert would have to say about that way of doing business, or a member of a labor union. But when we get Jesus' point, or points, it makes plenty of sense.

The story is told by Matthew (20:1–16). Let's get it in context first; that's always important.

This parable is the result of two conversations which were related in the preceding chapter.

a.) The rich young ruler had come and asked Jesus, "what good thing shall I do, that I may have eternal life?" (Matt. 19:16). He wanted to buy a place in heaven, or at least make a reservation there, with one specific act. But Jesus' answer sent him away sorrowful, for he thought the price was too high.

b.) After he had gone, Peter said, "Behold, we have forsaken all, and followed thee; what shall we have therefore?" (Matt. 19:27). In today's language, "What do we get out of it?"

Jesus didn't show any irritation, or even impatience. Peter just didn't know any better; none of them did. But he wanted them to understand, for there was a very important lesson involved here, so he told them a story.

In the story it was September, the time of grape harvest in Palestine. It was the critical time of year for any man who owned a vineyard, for his income for the next year depended on the successful harvesting of the grapes when they were at their peak. I judge it was often a time of worry, too, for the pickers were transients who had to be hired just when needed, not employed permanently. Besides the condition of the grapes, another thing set a deadline—the weather. At the end of September the rains came, and the grapes that hadn't been harvested would be ruined.

So the migrants would gather before dawn in the marketplaces of the towns and wait sometimes for hours, all day even, hoping to be hired, for their living, too, depended on the grape harvest. On some days, there would be more workers in the open-air employment centers than there were jobs, and some would have to go away empty-handed and heartsick to families who wouldn't get enough to eat that day. This group wasn't lazy, but unfortunate. Sometimes there wouldn't be enough workers, and then the householders would worry.

Jesus' hearers were, of course, perfectly familiar with this background. The householder in his story came to the marketplace five times that day, the first time very early, apparently at 6:00 A.M. He hired all the men he could, promised them what they asked, a denarius (fifteen cents), and took them to his vineyard. At 9:00 A.M. (the third hour) he went back again, found others waiting, and hired them. He did the same at noon, at 3:00 P.M, and at 5:00 P.M.

At 6:00 P.M. he said to his steward, "Call the men in and pay them the standard rate. Begin with the last group."

The first group began to get angry as soon as they saw the last group getting a day's pay, and their fury mounted as man by man the laborers were all paid the same amount. Finally they, too, received a denarius. They began to shout their protests; in fact, there was a near riot. But the owner stood his ground. Eccentric he might be, but he was not stupid! He had his position, and he knew exactly what it was. He had been fair to the first group, they had had no complaint, and he had paid them according to the bargain made with them. His generosity to others, he said, was no concern of theirs. It did not reduce their pay. He was the owner of the vineyard, the money was his, and what he did with it was his own business. They may have gone away grumbling, but they went, for they knew they had not been short-changed or mistreated. They just did not like to see others treated better—a very human trait, we will have to admit, but an ugly one.

In studying this parable, I found the answer to a puzzling question: why Jesus said, "The last shall be first and the first shall be last," and what he meant by it. I love the explanation! God, the householder, understood and pitied the worry of the eleventh hour workers who had gotten only one hour's work. Their wages would fall far short of the family's needs. So to relieve their anxiety at once, he said to the steward, "Give them a whole day's wages—and do it first."

When we have the whole situation in mind, we can see that Jesus was not concerned with labor-management relations, or with any economic principle. He wasn't talking about a materialistic society at all. He was trying to get a very important idea over to them, and ultimately to us: How very different are God's relations with men from men's with each other.

The kingdom of heaven operates on one principle—God's goodness. Those who truly work for him don't bargain, but trust him, as the eleventh-hour workers did. And he rewards us, not in proportion to what we earn, which would be only a pittance, but "above all that we are able to ask or think." I gather from things I read that many people try to make deals with God, saying, "If you'll just do this for me, I'll never ask for anything again." That reveals an ignorance about God that I find terribly pathetic.

His rewards, Jesus tells us here, are quite different from those of the world. God's ways and wages are not ours. In the kingdom, no value is put on money. The world's richest rewards are often unsatisfying, frequently ephemeral, sometimes carrying a drop of bitterness in their sweetest honey, and have to be given and received openly or they amount to little. God's rewards are permanent, enriching, satisfying; they need no advertising, may be cherished in secret, known only to the individual and God.

Sir Thomas More, a courageous churchman in a dangerous age, was consulted by a young man (Richard Rich) who was dazzled by the life at court, and thought of trying to get appointed to an office. Sir Thomas thought he should stick to the career for which he was fitted, which was education.

"But who would know?" asked the young man gloomily.

"Yourself, your pupils, your friends, and God—not a poor public," answered the churchman.

Most people who can do creative work of any sort would probably say that the monetary rewards are not the best part, even though they are important and may be necessary. I read something about Noah Webster recently. He wrote some books back in the late eighteenth and early nineteenth centuries, including some spellers, and so was considered an authority on the English language. He saw the need of a complete dictionary, and wanted to write it, but knew his scholarship was not adequate, so for ten years he studied English and other languages. Then the actual work took a long time, so he was seventy years old when *Webster's Dictionary* was finally published. Some ten years later, he saw revision was necessary; and though he was now more than eighty, he began that. When the last word was written, he wiped his quill pen, carefully straightened his desk, and walked across the room to his wife. He took her hand, said, "My dear, it is done," and knelt with her and thanked God.

He never kept track of the many hours he put in. Whatever money he may have received was not commensurate with the work he had done, but God paid him. His reward was the boundless satisfaction of making a great contribution to his country.

Satisfying, even creative, work doesn't depend on some spectacular talent. If it did, most of us would have to get our kicks cleaning and cooking.

On Christmas Eve, a woman died in Washington whom I had never heard of, but I read with interest an editorial about her in the *Washington Post.* She had been a telephone operator at the *Post* for fifty years. She had been so interested in her work, not only in efficient functioning at the switchboard but in the people she served and in those she served with, that she had lifted her work out of the job class and made it a career. She had given warmly and unstintingly of her own mental and spiritual resources when needed, so from a cog in a machine she became a personality, and the *Post* said she would be sorely missed. She fits perfectly into Jesus' story. She did not bargain with life, nor count in terms of dollars or hours what she gave to it, so life repaid her richly.

Now let's turn our attention to that first group of pickers. They don't impress us very favorably, do they? We see them as a pretty grabby set of people, decidedly selfish in their efforts to keep anyone from doing any better than they. What we should see is that in some respects we belong to that group, or at least have much in common, for they are prototypes of the largest segment of society. They weren't bad men. They were good workers, did an honest day's work. They had their standard, their code, but their fault was a lack of kindness, the inability to rejoice in good fortune they did not share.

But in the kingdom of heaven, that is a serious offense. Self-seeking as a way of life has no entrée there. They are like the self-righteous, unfeeling older brother of the prodigal son.

Mark Twain once described someone he knew as "a good man in the worst sense of the word." Jesus would have known exactly what he meant!

This seems to me an exceptionally timely parable. All through society from top to bottom people are obsessed with getting their rights—the right to happiness, leisure, money. . . . One doesn't have to be a marriage counselor to judge that failure of many marriages is simple selfishness, emphasis by one or both on getting their rights, on getting instead of giving. The wife is often afraid she won't get a proper share of her husband's income, or his time; afraid he'll do less for her family than for his. If both believe that loving means giving, marriage is the most perfect relationship on earth.

As we think about God's labor relations, we can't escape thinking about America's problems in that field. The labor unions have moved in the direction of the greed and indifference to the welfare of society which brought them into being in the first place. Many people who had a great deal of sympathy with the movement years ago have well-nigh lost it. The unions have focused on what they call their "rights" until they extend past where the public's rights begin.

Dr. Clarence Cranford, a well-known and much-beloved Baptist minister of Washington, D.C., received a letter from a union organizer asking him to join a union of ministers, stating that even ministers have to organize to get their rights. His answer was no—not that he was against unions, he said; quite the contrary. But as a minister, he had his rights—the right to witness, to worship, to serve, and he could exercise those rights without any union behind him.

I don't know any of Jesus' parables that would do more to change the world if understood and believed and followed than this one. If self-seeking were replaced by the Golden Rule, everybody would benefit and all would be a great deal happier.

*. . . the Indian Summer of life should be a
little sunny and a little sad, like the season,
and infinite in wealth and depth of tone . . .*
HENRY BROOKS ADAMS

What time I am afraid, I will trust in thee.
PSALM 56:3

13

Indian Summer
(October)

October is not just a span of thirty-one days.

It's the trees arrayed in gorgeous technicolor. It's damp leaves
on the pavement and blowing in the wind. It's pumpkins and
nuts and Winesap apples. For those who have gardens, it's the
time when the hard work has been done, and most of the ripening
can be left to Mother Nature.

At least, it was that way when I was young. Indian summer
was a season with dignity and authority of its own. My recollec-
tion is of wonderful spicey days that went to the head like wine,
a purplish haze over the Boston Mountains (some New England
hills that migrated to Arkansas), crimson leaves on the sweet
gum trees, and purple grapes on the table. It came after the
agony of summer, our ordeal by heat, was over. And it was
the way summer should be—a time of pure enchantment—but
never was!

Perhaps the soul has seasons, too. If so, I think its Indian
summer is meant to be, and can be, one of life's most pleasant
seasons. The hard work, the disciplining of the mind and body,

has been done; the ripening process is well on the way; and the perfecting and finishing of the fruits can be left to the Gardener.

Seneca has said about the later years, "As for old age, embrace it and love it. It abounds with pleasure if you know how to use it. The gradually (I do not say rapidly) declining years are among the sweetest in a man's life; and I maintain that even where they have reached the extreme limit, they have their pleasure still."

I daresay the same thing holds true for women! Our birthdays, then, are not our enemies but our friends, for after all we're still here!

Someone asked an elderly man, "Uncle Johnnie, what do you consider the best days of your life? When you were a boy, I suppose."

"No they were not!" the old man snapped. "The best days are today and tomorrow."

With a philosophy like that, who needs youth? And a philosophy is exactly what we do need to help us to adapt gracefully to the changes the years bring.

The physical signs of age are perhaps hardest on women, although the struggle of some men to hold on to their hair is pathetic. A silly woman who was a belle at the French court of Louis XIV decided she wanted to be remembered at the height of her beauty, so when she was only thirty-two years old she left the court and entered a convent. She was not interested in a religious life; she merely chose it as the lesser of two evils. She was probably better off away from that corrupt court, but one can only wonder how she fitted into the life of the convent, especially if she continued to be obsessed by thoughts of her face.

One sign of maturity is to be able to give material and physical things their proper value.

I think, however, that Fannie Holmes was not being unreasonable when her husband, Oliver Wendell, told her he had been appointed to the Supreme Court. He thought she would be excited and pleased, and maybe she was, at first. But she soon had a sobering second thought. "Just look at me! How can I go to Washington? I look like an abandoned farm in Maine!" (told by Catherine Drinker Bowen in *Adventures of a Biographer*).

If Thomas Aquinas could pray, "Help me to grow old without growing dull," women should certainly be permitted, without being charged with frivolity, to resolve not to look like abandoned farms no matter how old we get!

When the movies and I were young, I had a crush on Billie Burke. She was only a girl herself, but had become a bright star on Broadway and was beginning to act for the silver screen. One of her first pictures was a serial called *Gloria's Romance*.

My sister and I, equipped with the ticket price of ten cents, went every Saturday for several weeks and sat enthralled in the one little movie theater in Fort Smith watching that lovely, graceful girl.

I never saw her in person until a short time before her death. It was in the National Airport in Washington. She was with a young woman and was holding a child by the hand. She was wearing a sky-blue suit with a bunch of violets on the lapel, and I thought her as lovely as ever. I stopped in my tracks and gawked like some rustic from the sticks until she was lost in the crowd. When I told my husband I had just seen Billie Burke, he said as skeptically as if I had claimed to have seen Hamlet's father's ghost, "You're kidding."

The next day I was vindicated, for an item in the newspaper reported that she had been here. A taxi driver recognized her when she stepped into his cab, turned around and asked, "Aren't you Miss Billie Burke?"

She had answered with a sigh, "What's left of her."

Well, there was a lot left! If she could have seen herself through my eyes, she would not have been depressed but delighted; for I saw through the superficial changes to the characteristics I remembered in the girl. The features were the same—the curly gray hair was as attractive as the brown hair had been and the sweet expression of the mouth was as charming as ever.

What is left when we reach Indian summer should be the best part of any of us, the part we have been cultivating—if we are wise—for years. We should prepare our minds for the many changes the passing years will bring by adopting a philosophy of expectation and acceptance while trusting in a loving God who understands. To go into the afternoon of life expecting every day to be full of sunshine, blind to the possibility that rain or tears may fall, is to invite depression and cynicism. I have read of people who were so stunned by misfortune or sorrow that they were shaken to pieces by it. One woman, furious because fate had dealt her a blow, cried angrily, "I shall have something to say to God!" We should not at any time of life have an It-can't-happen-to-me attitude, but we should expect crises and prepare in advance to handle them with poise and courage. "Quiet minds," said Robert Louis Stevenson, "cannot be perplexed or frightened, but go on in fortune or misfortune at their own private pace like a clock ticking in a thunderstorm."

I once saw a poor train conductor harassed by a nervous passenger. My husband and I were on the National Limited going to St. Louis where we had to change trains for Washington. We had lost an hour or so due to a hot box and were going to be late. A woman sitting across from us was in knots. Every time the conductor went through the car she stopped him, and tried to get a guarantee from him that the Washington train would wait. He must have wanted to choke her! Then, finding that Brooks was sympathetic, she used him as a wailing wall. He had to practically hold her hand for the last hour! I was in knots, too, but I had to soothe myself. Hers were so much worse that I was about as important as a toothache in the same room with a concussion.

That was a very insignificant crisis, as such things go. I wonder how that woman would meet a real one. We are our own worst enemies when we suffer in advance over what may not happen, or waste our nervous energy instead of conserving it till it is really needed. "[Your anxiety] does not empty tomorrow, brother, of its sorrow; but ah! it empties today of its strength" (Ian MacLaren).

When we think of a perfectly controlled and adjusted life, one without fear, we think of Jesus. He didn't fray his nerves with worry over what might happen. He could lie down and go to sleep in an open boat on a rough sea in the face of a gathering storm. He could relax when he needed rest and sleep peacefully until awakened. He was at peace with himself.

He was also at peace with life. He didn't complain about it, or rail at it, or bewail its imperfections as we often do. He not only accepted it, he loved it, met it joyously and radiantly, and wanted it abundantly for everyone. We too can cultivate an enjoyment of life for its own sake.

A mother said to her small daughter, "Look at your feet, Winkle! Why is it that you look like a coal heaver at the end of every day? What do you *do?*"

"I just live," said Winkle serenely. "Living is dirty work, but I like it."

How right! God gave us life to enjoy. I think he is pleased when we say at night, "Lord, this has been such a lovely day." We may not have done anything but putter in the yard and discover a crocus in bloom, take a walk in the warm sunshine, exchange greetings with a friend, or enjoy a good book. Even on the days when the sun doesn't shine if we are really at peace with life, we'll accept its storms without bitterness and resentment, realizing that it's a great and precious gift.

John Wesley wrote on the flyleaf of his Bible, "Live today!" For myself, I believe I'd like to make that motto, "Enjoy today."

The world knows the story of Anne Frank—her family lived in concealed rooms in a house in Amsterdam until they were discovered by Nazis and sent to a concentration camp where Anne died. A year earlier, she had written in her diary: "Nearly every morning I go to the attic. . . . From my favorite spot on the floor I look up at the blue sky. . . . 'As long as this exists,' I thought, 'and I may live to see it, this sunshine, the cloudless skies, while this lasts I cannot be unhappy'. . . .

"Riches can all be lost, but that happiness in your own heart can only be veiled, and it will still bring you happiness again as long as you live. As long as you can look fearlessly up into the heavens. . . ." *

At fifteen years of age, that young girl had a mature philosophy which a woman of eighty might envy.

Jesus was at peace with God. His own words give the most complete explanation of that, "I do always those things that please him" (John 8:29). And we know what those things are, for they are summed up in two commandments.

When Titov, the Russian astronaut, was asked, "Did you see God? Did you see any angels?" he answered, "I saw no God and no angels." That was predictable. The question was asked of a skeptic by skeptics. It reminds me of Jacob who, though a primitive man by scientific standards, was wiser and more perceptive than the Russian space-age specialists. For after an experience a great deal simpler than Titov's, he said, "Surely God was in this place, and I knew it not." Sensing God's presence depends on the individual's spiritual maturity.

If we have disciplined our spirits, if patience has wrought her perfect work, if we have learned to trust God so completely that we can take with tranquility whatever comes, then the Indian summer of the soul should be a season of happiness and fulfillment.

* B. M. Mooyaart-Doubleday, trans., *Anne Frank: The Diary of a Young Girl* (Garden City, N.Y.: Doubleday & Company, Inc., 1952), pp. 171–72.

When the fight begins within himself,
A man's worth something.
ROBERT BROWNING

As thy days, so shall thy strength be.
DEUTERONOMY 33:25

14

Haunted Houses
(Halloween)

Because I believe we never outgrow our enjoyment of Halloween and a mild flavor of horror, I'm going to repeat the ghost story Jesus told, and try to interpret it as I think he meant us to. In the spirit of the season, I will call it "Haunted Houses." Luke tells it in chapter 11.

Some ghosts are benevolent, kindly old souls that come back to warn those on earth, like Jacob Marley's ghost. But the one in Jesus' story was a mean spirit. The man who had been giving him house room finally had enough and evicted him, and then went to work and cleaned the empty apartment. He enjoyed the wonderful feeling of being clean and wholesome and righteous again and resolved there would be no more drinking, carousing, and bad companions. He had the best of intentions, but he put off taking any constructive steps.

Meanwhile, the bad spirit, finding no place to lodge, said to himself, "I'll just go 'round and see if my old apartment is still vacant." So he went around, and lucky for him no one was in it, no one at all, and it had been redecorated! So he just went in and took it over. It was as simple as that.

Feeling the occasion called for a celebration, he went out again and rounded up seven of his cronies, ribald, vulgar fellows even more noisy and uninhibited than himself, and invited them in for a housewarming. Once in there, they stayed, and the last state of that house was worse than the first.

I think they all laughed as Jesus finished, and that he meant for them to, that he told it with a twinkle in his eye. But they didn't forget, and they may have had some very sober thoughts as they went away, for the little story had a very big truth in it.

In the words of an English author, George Robert Sims, "The law of life is movement toward a purpose. Whenever civilization pauses in its march of conquest, it is over-thrown by the barbarian." That was exactly what Jesus said, only he used devils. The devils can be many things. One is physical decay. That nature abhors a vacuum is one of the first lessons we learn in natural science.

Once in Panama my husband and I were taken to see the ruins of an ancient city, once the capital, built by the Spaniards under Cortez. At some time in the long past, a horde of Indian or native tribes took the city by surprise and conquered it, then returned to their native villages leaving the ravaged city to molder and decay. When we saw it, it looked like a graveyard with old pillars and building stones for monuments—and that's what it was, the graveyard of a civilization. The barbarian had taken possession.

There are other and subtler applications of Jesus' story. When man pauses in his struggle to conquer disease, poverty, ignorance and sin he loses ground. Wherever there is emptiness, idleness, laziness, weakness or apathy the barbarian takes over. When an individual pauses in his moral and spiritual growth a devil, or a whole bunch, moves in.

Jesus' story and the law of life it illustrates make it plain why we can't win freedom once for all and sit down and enjoy it. Much surprise was expressed, some of it sarcastic, when we had to fight a second time "to make the world safe for democracy." When Mussolini was asked to explain his spectacular rise to power, he said, "I found Europe a continent of empty thrones. I simply went in and sat down on one of them."

When we came marching home from Germany, pretty self-satisfied, after World War I, we should not have been so complacent. Jesus' warning could not have been more applicable to that situation. We had exorcised an evil spirit, true. Germany was swept and garnished; the Kaiser, his armies, German militarism—all swept into the dust heap. The world was now safe! Some people did say, "But we aren't through, yet! We must see that peace comes to live there."

But the majority were opposed. "That would take years! No, we've done enough." So we cleared out, leaving Germany empty. And there were devils just waiting to move in—hatred of non-Germans, resentment against the conquerors, bitterness over their humiliation, a burning desire for revenge. And the last state of that house was worse than the first. It was ripe for Hitler. The barbarian came and took over. "It wasn't that the knife was so sharp but that the cheese was so soft." There was no stability and no moral fiber. Just an empty place.

A heartening illustration of how this immutable fact of life can work in our favor is recorded by Dr. Frank Laubach in *The Silent Billion Speak*. He said the loyalty of the Philippine people to the United States, at a time (World War II) when other dependent people were turning against their overlords has amazed the world. He reviewed a little history for us. At the end of the Spanish-American War, the Philippines fell to the United States as a minor consequence. In a fever of idealism the U.S. government sent doctors and teachers to this newly acquired land. The churches sent missionaries. We made mistakes, but we made the welfare of the people and not exploitation of them our object. This is the first and only time in history, he said, that a dominant power gave more consideration to educating a people than to exploiting them. We sent thousands of American teachers, and we raised the literacy level from 5 percent to 75 percent in forty-four years. Every now and then, this old blundering nation that seems to make so many mistakes, and can never seem to pull together except in war when we're scared to death, does something so fine and worthy that it surprises even itself. We might have pulled out after that war and left those benighted islands to shift for themselves. But they had no idea of self-government and would have been like a rudderless ship. Instead, we created something there, something fine and true and good.

And then after Pearl Harbor when we were at bay, we found, instead of a house haunted by devils which would have turned on us to rend us, a country of friends who came to our rescue, who in their gratitude were loyal to us even to the point of sacrificing themselves.

Now let's see what Jesus was teaching about discipleship. We realize at once he was saying he requires a positive, not a negative, approach to life and its problems. His was *not* that of nonviolence, a negative policy. His followers must *overcome* evil by applying a stronger force, the force of love. "Go the second mile," he told them. "Turn the other cheek. Give more than you are asked. Love your enemies. Forgive a slight seventy times seven." Even while we are getting rid of a bad habit, we must invite in a virtue to take its place.

Cicero, a Roman philosopher who lived one hundred years or so before Jesus, wrote a charming little book called *De Amicitia*. At least, I am told it is charming, but I had to read it in the original (in Sophomore Latin), translating as I went, so its charm escaped me. He did write eloquently about the sentiment shared by friends. It did not extend to those Cicero did not like. He once dated a letter, "The 566th day," meaning since he had paid off a grudge. It had been nearly two years, and he was still gloating. He had never heard of forgiving one's enemies.

At that time, even the Jews held to the old philosophy of an eye for an eye. Not until Jesus came with a new doctrine, that the way to overcome evil was not by force but by love, was such an idea ever heard of, and the world was slow to accept it. But the world's way of repaying hate with hate is the impractical, ineffectual way, the way to keep enemies. Unless, one is like the old man who lived to be ninety and was interviewed on his birthday, as if by virtue of having lived so long he was suddenly endowed with divine wisdom, when it was known to all his acquaintances that he was a mean old coot. "Do you have any enemies?" the reporter asked.

He thought a minute, then said, "Nope. Nary a one."

"Well! How do you account for that?"

He threw back his head with a squeaky chortle. "I've just outlived all the old polecats!"

That way of dealing with enemies is not only too chancy, but makes Christians polecats as much as anybody else!

The world was very slow to accept the idea that love is not weak and futile but very, very powerful, and that hatred and physical force are self-defeating. Even now, when we accept it in theory, we are slow to trust it and reluctant to commit ourselves fully. A phrase in a play by Sophocles, the Greek dramatist, comes to my mind. He named the play, which he wrote in 443 B.C. during the Golden Age, for his heroine, *Antigone*. The story, briefly, is this:

When the King of Thebes, Oedipus, died, according to his decree his two sons were to rule alternately, a year at a time. The elder son, Antiocles, ruled first. Then it was Polyneices' turn, but Antiocles refused to step down and yield the scepter to his brother. Polyneices was infuriated. He selected seven loyal friends, raised an army and marched against Thebes. (That battle became the theme of another play by Sophocles, *The Seven Against Thebes*.)

After a long siege and much fighting without getting anywhere, it was decided that twelve men from each side should fight it out. These twenty-four were all killed, so they were back where they started; but others carried on the fight until both brothers were killed, and a relative seized the throne. As he had been a supporter of Antiocles, he decreed that Polyneices' body should not be buried. That was the extreme punishment, for to the Greeks it was comparable to destroying the soul.

Now Polyneices had two sisters, Antigone and Ismene, who desperately wanted to bury their brother, but while Antigone was determined to carry it out in defiance of the state, Ismene tried to dissuade her.

"We're only women. We are not men. The obligations of such heroism do not descend upon us."

Antigone scorned that reasoning, so Ismene tried again. "Think how we shall perish if we defy the state."

"I'll not urge thee, Ismene. Nay, be thou what thou wilt. But I shall bury my brother. I owe a larger allegiance to the dead than to the living."

Ismene, wringing her hands: "I do them no dishonor. But defy the state! I have no strength for that."

Both Ismene and Antigone have counterparts today, as in every age. Sophocles' point was that there are times when the state is wrong and should be defied. The young men who sincerely believed that the Vietnam war was wrong, and left their native land rather than engage in it, could have found support not only in Antigone but in St. Peter, who defied the state when he had to choose between obedience to it or God (Acts 5:17–32).

But such choices do not often confront the average Christian. We frequently meet simple situations, however, where moral courage is needed. Society is burdened by some traditions and ideas which have become shibboleths, so hoary and hidebound they are like Longfellow's pines and hemlocks, "bearded with eld." Some are supported by ancient prejudices and outmoded social patterns which run directly counter to the Sermon on

the Mount. We are aware of that, yet to defy them we would
have to go counter to our friends. All too often we have no
strength for that.

Some years ago when the Little Rock school desegregation
problem had our city in turmoil and my husband as their repre-
sentative in the Congress risked his seat (and lost it) to try to
persuade them to comply with the law, a preacher friend said
to him, "Brooks, let me give you a little advice—stay out of
all hot spots. They don't do you any good. And it's all over
nothing."

At that last sentence, I could feel my jaw drop. I had raised
my foot to step into our car, and I nearly fell under it. As we
drove off, I said, "Did he say *it's all over nothing?*"

Brooks, very grimly, answered, "That's what he said."

Strange advice from a minister who interprets for others the
teachings of Jesus! Jesus appeals to the strength in us, not the
weakness.

The late Dr. R. W. Hudgens of Chapel Hill, North Carolina,
has written an eloquent testimonial to the memory of the revered
and beloved Frank Graham, former president of the University
of North Carolina. He said he knew Frank Graham long before
he met him, because of the enemies Dr. Graham had made.
"They had colored him a washed-out red, only they called it
pink. . . . What went through my mind as I first listened to
Frank Graham was a feeling of fascination over what showed
through of his inner self. Where was his battleground, I wondered, for people are not born with strength to do what he
had done, people don't win merely by being gentle and patient,
and they don't go into tough battles with untested spiritual mus-
cles. I thought to myself: this man's dedication hasn't come
easy—somewhere, sometime, he has fought and won tough battles that only *he* knew about, that lesser men would have lost.
Sometime, maybe many times, he had fought battles with himself
that he did not win, and maybe *there* was the muscular strength
of his commitment. Something had taught him to be triumphant

even when he didn't win but lost. . . . Frank Graham never either won or lost a battle, alone or in company, that has not raised human worth and dignity a little level higher than it would have reached if he had not been here."

This brings to mind a quote I heard years ago, from a source which I cannot remember: "Earth might be fair . . . would man but wake from out his haunted sleep."

15

Day of Remembrance
(Thanksgiving)

Thanksgiving, like most other times of religious observance in our national life, is a good time to look backward to our national origins and think gratefully of our forefathers—those first refugees who came with such high hopes to found on this continent a new nation, conceived in liberty. A time to remember the traditions which set the pattern for our unique celebration, for Thanksgiving Day belongs to us Americans as a family. It is a time when our hearts turn in gratitude to God, as theirs did, for his goodness, patience and love. A solemn time.

But it is also a joyous time, and so we feast, as they did. Like other good things, it can be overdone, and some will keep Thanksgiving quite simply by overeating, topped off with a ball game.

Benjamin Franklin is said to have written in a letter to a friend that he would like to return from his grave in about one hundred years, and have "a little look around." It is natural that he would like to see what was happening in the republic he helped found. If he were to show up on the last Thursday in November, he might be surprised at the degree to which the roasted turkeys outnumber the worshipers at church services, and bewildered at the hordes of Americans watching a little pigskin being kicked around a field. He might be pardoned for thinking that activity was the purpose and focus of the day.

I like to look back as far as my memory permits, some seventy-odd years (very odd some of them were, too). That's quite a distance, but I can't remember the arrival of the Pilgrims! I have lots of nostalgic but happy memories connected with celebrations of this day in my childhood. These were mostly at school. I remember several years when my room gave a little play on the Wednesday before Thanksgiving, with our mothers sitting in the back of the room, a sympathetic and most uncritical audience, watching their little girls in tissue paper caps and fichus, and their little boys wearing either pasteboard hats and shoe buckles or Indian headdresses. Some of the comically youthful Pilgrim Fathers must have amused the teachers. I don't know whether the mothers would have been so alert to the comic aspect of the situation.

The walls on these occasions would be decorated with our best artistic efforts—overripe pumpkins and scrawny, anemic turkeys—and there would be a really respectable pile of canned food and sacks of fruit and vegetables in one corner, our room's Thanksgiving offering. That was important because those were the days before there was any United Givers' Fund.

The amount of history I learned on those occasions was small and may not have been strictly accurate, but I did gain there my strongest impressions about the magnificent courage of the Pilgrims, their sustaining faith and endurance during their first hard years, and the friendliness and hospitality shown to the Indians.

The first time I crossed the Atlantic by boat I realized more than ever the sheer physical courage it took to set sail on pirate-infested seas in what, by contrast with our huge liners, were frail barks. There is an old pier on the coast of Amsterdam in

Holland which has a round brick tower called the Weeping Place. It is the place where the *Mayflower*, and later the *Due Return* and the *True Love* set out. It doesn't take much imagination to picture the scenes. Partings were just as hard in those days as now, and a great deal more final. When a mother told her daughter good-bye, she didn't know whether she would ever see her again. Much sorrow went into the founding of this nation. Among the ingredients were tears. Then when they reached these shores there were other hardships they hadn't expected; they didn't anticipate the long severe winters and the barren soil. And some of the Indians were far from friendly.

If a small group of Pilgrim fathers and mothers could come back now, some 350 years later, to have "a little look around," wouldn't it be a fascinating experience to get their reactions? Imagine them at a big airport! The open mouths, dropped jaws, bugging eyes. They would exclaim, "How do they dare!" forgetting their own bravery.

Gratitude is the emotion which governs and sanctifies this season, the thing that lifts it out of the secular and carnal and makes it a religious holiday. But our gratitude to the Puritans has its limitations. We are grateful to them for coming, for their ideal of religious freedom, for their unswerving belief in God; but we are not grateful for their joyless worship, their distrust of beauty, their intolerant authoritarian interpretations. Tragically, they betrayed their own dream of religious liberty— of divorcing the State and the Church so neither would have power over the other, of denying the divine right of very human kings. For this dream they were willing to give up the comforts of civilization and come to a raw, untamed land. As Hervey Allen expressed it in *The Forest and the Fort*, they deliberately disinherited themselves, the only time in history such a thing was done by a group of people. We accord them great honor for that.

And then when they got here what did they do? They fell right back into the old ways with the difference that *they* became the intolerant authorities, often fanatical and sometimes cruel to those who dared to defy them, like the heartless Archbishop Laud who had made their lives intolerable in England. They came to America as rebels against entrenched authority and then conducted themselves in such a way as to breed rebellion. It was the rebels *against* the Puritans who are the more outstanding heroes and heroines, men and women of amazing courage such as Roger Williams, Thomas Hooker and Anne Hutchinson. When the magistrates of the Massachusetts Bay Colony ordered the clergy to tell the people on the next Sunday that the Voice of the Magistrate was the Voice of God (since church attendance was compulsory, that was the quickest way to get the news around), those three said, "Nothing doing! We left England to escape the fallacy of the divine right of kings. We came to this country for a new freedom—freedom of conscience. Our government is to be the servant of the people, not the master." These three should never be forgotten, for they were true heroes of the faith. They were the radicals of their day, the nonconformists. They were shamed, disgraced, even persecuted, because they did not fit the pattern, and refused to adjust to the majority because they knew the pattern was wrong.

We can see now how right they were. But if we had belonged to the church at Salem or at Plymouth, would we have been with the dissidents, or against them? Or discreetly silent?

We wonder not only at the mistakes and inconsistencies of the Puritans but also at their distrust of beauty and pleasure.

Some years ago I read an interesting magazine article entitled "The Eatings of Conscience" by Bertha Damon. A descendent of seven *Mayflower* passengers, the author says she thinks it is curious that Puritan New England should have had such good eating; for the pleasures of eating are very great, and the Puritan was afraid of pleasure. The one kind of worldly pleasure he permitted himself and his family was eating and drinking. Even rum was not frowned upon, and the clergy were sometimes paid in kegs of it. But he regarded almost all other kinds of pleasure as pitfalls which would trap him in his arduous journey through this life to the Celestial City. So he made laws against all other forms of worldly pleasure, and created a grim god in his own image who joined him in frowning upon merriment and joy. The article also included a few instances from old records.

One of these was about Joshua Lewis and Sarah Chapman who were arrested and fined for sitting under the apple tree in somebody's orchard on the Lord's Day. (That could have been the inspiration for a song with a title like "Don't sit under the apple tree with anybody—it ain't safe," but I doubt if it would have "played" in New England!)

In Salem, a man who had been at sea for two years unfortunately got home on Sunday and kissed his wife before he realized it was the Sabbath. He was fined.

Weekday life wasn't much more fun. Bearbaiting was popular, but was banned by the magistrates, not because of the pain it gave the bear but the pleasure it gave the spectators.

Judge Sewell of Boston wrote in his diary in 1715 that he went out at night on horseback to inspect the town. He suspected there would be goings-on, and he was right. He found a group of men and boys playing nine pins on "Mt. Whoredom," broke up the game and sent them home. No fines. He must have been feeling good! His editor explains in a footnote, "We may presume this spot to have been on the slope of Beacon Hill."

Then, of course, they were afraid of beautiful or rich clothing and any sort of adornment. A Reverend Mr. Ward wrote hotly about the evil effects of fashion on women—and also on him: "To speak moderately, I . . . truly confess that it is beyond my . . . understanding to conceive how [some] women . . . have so little wit as to disfigure themselves with such exotic garbs. . . . It is no marvel they wear Drailies [trailing headdresses] on the hinder part of their heads; having nothing, it seems, in the forepart but a few squirrel's brains to help them frisk from one ill-favored Fashion to another." And then the Reverend Mr. Ward adds with unconscious self-revelation, "We have about five or six of them in our Colony; if I see any of them accidentally, I cannot cleanse my fancy of them for a month after."

I think he proved the efficacy of adornment for women.

In view of all this, the Puritan attitude toward food and drink was strangely inconsistent, but somehow the gullet was sanctified. For this inconsistency may the Lord make us truly thankful.

We have learned much since those days about the nature and heart of God.

An idea for a story he never got around to writing was found among F. Scott Fitzgerald's papers after he died. It concerned a will which left a valuable house to members of a family which had scattered and grown apart. There was a condition—they all had to return home and live together in the house. That plot certainly contained possibilities for drama. Anything could have happened, from mayhem to murder. But on the other hand, if each respected the rights of others, if they were all kind and considerate of one another, the house could have become a real home, a haven of rest and comfort for all, a refuge from the stress and strains of living.

That's what God did when he gave us the world. Such a beautiful home, with gardens, lakes and rivers, hills and trees, flowers and birds. But we have never fully realized its great potentialities for blessing and happiness. We've never really inherited the earth because we've never learned to live harmoniously together. One thing to be thankful for on this and every Thanksgiving day is our belief that God loves the world. One of the great mistakes the Puritans made was that they condemned the world.

Pride of ancestry sometimes masquerades as gratitude. At a small college that had an annual Thanksgiving dinner, it was customary to have a few short talks from the faculty and students on what they were grateful for. A professor spoke at some length on how grateful he was for his American ancestry—his forefathers on both sides of the family had come over on the *Mayflower* (or so he said).

He was followed by a student, who said, "I am a first generation

American. Both my parents were born in Europe. But I too can be proud of their arrival in this country, for when my parents came the immigration authorities were a lot stricter than when the ancestors of the good professor arrived."

I think the inimitable Will Rogers, who could not bear snobbishness, delivered the *coup de grace* on this subject when he said to a well-known women's organization, "When your ancestors arrived, mine were on the shore to meet them."

Our Day of Remembrance. Just one day in which to remember and to be grateful for all God's gifts? I hope not. Rather, it's just a little reminder, like a red circle on the calendar. A character in *How Green Was My Valley* by Richard Llewellyn asked, "What if God were to reach his hand down out of the clouds and present a bill?"

That's a shocking idea. If he did do such a thing, we would be even more shocked by the size of the bill, for it would contain many items we take for granted and for which we seldom spare a grateful thought. Free air (which if no longer 100 percent pure is not his fault), sunlight and birds' songs, water, trees, sleep. . . . So many things we never pay for! Papa's bills on the first of the month would be nothing to it.

One of the most scintillating occurrences in Great Britain's illustrious history was the celebration in London in 1898 of Queen Victoria's sixty-year reign, the Diamond Jubilee. People came from all the dominions, wearing their own colorful costumes, carrying bright banners, bringing their native animals to march in a spectacular parade. There were elephants from India, camels and other exotic beasts from the other dominions. All the countries represented were bound together by one common tie— they were all subservient to England, all the victims of conquest. The cheering throngs who watched the magnificent parade from balconies, windows and curbsides were proud of the far-flung empire on which the sun never set.

But there was one person who saw it all in a different light. A little unimportant poet named Rudyard Kipling was asked to write a poem commemorating the event. He knew what they wanted—a poem extolling the military and material greatness of Britain. It was a fine chance for him. It would certainly add to his prestige. He made many starts but all ended in the wastebasket. He could not bring himself to write the boasts which he saw as false. It was a fine display for Britain, but what about the feelings of the conquered peoples? How much were they enjoying the exhibition of their dominated status? Perhaps that question was in Kipling's mind. Finally, he gave up the struggle; he had had his moment of truth. He decided he must be honest and true to himself. And so Kipling wrote one of the great poems in the English language, "Recessional." I quote two of the five verses:

> God of our fathers, known of old,
>   Lord of our far-flung battle-line,
> Beneath whose awful Hand we hold
>   Dominion over palm and pine—
> Lord God of Hosts, be with us yet,
> Lest we forget—lest we forget!
>
> The tumult and the shouting dies;
>   The Captains and the Kings depart:
> Still stands Thine ancient sacrifice,
>   An humble and a contrite heart.
> Lord God of Hosts, be with us yet,
> Lest we forget—lest we forget!

We do indeed need a special thanksgiving day, for we have so much to remember!

16

Tidings of Joy
(Christmas)

The "Spirit of Christmas" is such a lovely phrase. It evokes all sorts of delightful sights, like holly wreaths upon front doors, animated scenes in store windows, fairylike gift wrappings, stars and candlelight.

It brings to the memory sounds, too—of carols and of happy voices saying, "Merry Christmas!" Delicious smells are also associated with Christmas—the odor of evergreens in the house, the wonderful mixed bouquet of the kitchen.

But these things, delightful as they are, are the tinsel and surface trappings. The Spirit of Christmas is a great and wonderful force which operates powerfully on many people. Not everyone believes in it, of course; there are people like Ebenezer Scrooge, who pronounced it a "humbug." He didn't want to believe in Christmas for he was a thoroughly selfish person. It would require something of him, and he didn't want to give anything. And so he called it phony and tried to deny its existence.

But we know it is real because of what it does. For a few

weeks it works many miracles. Practical, unsentimental people often become soft-hearted, even soft-headed! The most self-centered ones may feel a stirring of brotherly love that lifts them above their usual selves. Rich and poor clasp hands, remembering their brotherhood, and strangers are drawn together by the exchange of a smile or friendly greeting and go away warm and uplifted.

The Christmas Spirit is composed of several elements, and one of these is *joy.* The angel made that clear: "For, behold, I bring you good tidings of great joy." I am so glad he did, for throughout history some religious people have been afraid of joy and regarded it as sinful. We all feel, rightly, that too much emphasis may be put on unimportant things at this season, but one of these is not joy. True, deep, basic happiness is our Christian heritage, for the birth of Jesus brought more joy into the world than it had ever known. We have a song by Isaac Watts that tells the story, a carol of rich and buoyant melody:

> Joy to the world; the Lord is come;
> Let earth receive her King;
> Let ev'ry heart prepare him room,
> And heav'n and nature sing.

What a pity that some others besides Scrooge don't feel that joy and don't experience the glow which participation in it bestows!

When I was shopping one December day, I heard a woman say to her companion, "I shocked my children last night by saying I wished I could sleep right through Christmas and wake up when it was all over!" I should think it would shock them. I thought it was terrible myself. It would have spoiled Christmas for me if my mother had ever said anything like that.

One thing that stands out in my memories of the Christmases of my childhood is Mother's pleasure in her simple preparations. When you don't have much money you have to fall back on

ingenuity, and on talent if you have it. Mother had a talent—
she could paint—but for years she had little time to indulge
it. So the season opened officially for me when Mother got out
her paints, and I distinguished those Christmases by what Mother
painted that year. In my early childhood, it was china; then
that went out of style, and we went out of money. In very
lean years it was a sachet to hold some handkerchiefs, or a little
unframed watercolor with a calendar pasted beneath and a ribbon
at the top to hold it on the wall.

There were several old ladies on our street—my grandmother's
set—and Mother always made something for them. One year
she bought small milk pitchers at the newly opened Kress store
(our first five-and-ten) and filled them with homemade candy.
My little sister and I thought everything she did was wonderful,
and we loved our job of taking them to their destinations on
Christmas Eve.

Those who find Christmas so burdensome, and indeed all of
us, would do well to try to get back some of the simplicity of
the old days; but certainly any pattern of celebration that pre-
cludes joy should be changed. Perhaps our inflated economy
will give us a push in that direction.

On another occasion when I was doing some shopping alone,
I went to the tearoom of our largest department store for lunch.
It was crowded, and I was shown to a table for two where a
woman was already sitting. After she finished, a man asked if
he might sit there. I said, "Certainly. I'm just leaving anyway."

"Please—not on my account. I like someone to sit with me
while I eat." (Maybe I'm not so old as I thought.) I didn't
feel I could take on that responsibility—he had quite a tray
full—but at least I didn't hurry. We talked about Christmas.
He said, "We've solved the problem at our house—my wife
and I don't give each other anything."

I blurted out, "Oh, my! What my husband gives me is the
most important thing I get!"

"Is it?" He looked a further question, and I said, "Not a

mink coat, nor anything like it. It may not be the biggest or the most expensive, but it will be the best."

What we give each other belongs by right to the Spirit of the day, and is not expendable, for it is given with love.

I read a poignant human interest story in some periodical one December. A little waif, trying to sell something to hurrying shoppers on Christmas Eve, was knocked down on the icy street and injured. She was taken to the charity ward of a big city hospital where the doctors and nurses who fixed her up, seeing her emaciated frame, called her Little Broomstick.

The next day was the happiest of her life. Early in the morning she was awakened by the sound of carols. Then a trimmed and lighted Christmas tree was brought in by members of a Sunday School class who took care of this ward and made Christmas Day a delight. Then dinner. Little Broomstick ate delicious things she had never tasted before and didn't know the names of. In the afternoon a lovely gray-haired lady sat by her bed and told her why we celebrate Christmas. She had never heard of Jesus before.

After the lady had gone, Little Broomstick gave a happy sigh and said to the discontented-looking young nurse, "When I get well, I will have to leave this beautiful place. But I can take Jesus with me. I never will be alone any more." Then, timidly, to the nurse, "I guess you didn't know about Jesus either, did you?"

The young nurse, disappointed at not getting the afternoon off, spoke more sharply than she meant to. "Certainly I know. Why do you say that?"

Little Broomstick flushed. "Because—you didn't look happy."

Amelia, a character in *The Late George Apley* by John P. Marquand, said, "Whenever I am depressed, I remember I am an Apley."

It's hard to understand how a name bestowed by the accident of birth could be so potent. To remember we are Christians is a great deal more sensible, especially if we remember who we are during the December rush. It would do more than anything to remove the shameful odium attached to the term "Christmas shoppers."

A little Jewish clerk was injured in a store in the Christmas rush and was taken to a hospital. She had been told it was "a Christian hospital." Looking up at the kind face of the nurse whose hand rested so gently on her forehead, she said, "Are you really a Christian?"

"Why, yes, Jennie. Why?"

"I can't believe anyone so sweet and polite as you could be. But then all the Christians I have known were Christmas shoppers."

I myself overheard a conversation at one of our big department stores in Washington one December. I was waiting at the gift-wrapping desk and heard one of the clerks say to another, her hands never pausing in their quick work, "Yes, sir. She collapsed right here at this desk, lost her mind in the elevator, and they took her straight to Gallinger [a mental hospital]."

Perfectly solemnly, the other clerk answered, "That's the way I'm going."

I think the fault is sometimes in the feet instead of the heart. I saw an ad in the paper containing the warning, "There are still 66 *shopping miles* until Christmas." The same item said the average shopper trudges eleven miles a day during the season, and added, "That woman with the pained expression and all the bundles isn't really cross. It's just that her feet are killing her." In many cases, the Spirit is there, but the feet are weak!

To tuck Whittier's words ("The Joy of Giving") away in our minds as a little talisman, to help us remember we are Christian shoppers, would be a good idea:

> For somehow, not only at Christmas
> But all the long year through,
> The joy that you give to others
> Is the joy that comes back to you.

To know the deep and solemn joy of Christmas, it may be that we must first seek the *peace* which is another element of the Spirit of Christmas. That, too, was in the heavenly message delivered to the shepherds. "And suddenly there was with the angel a multitude of the heavenly host praising God, and saying, Glory to God in the highest, and on earth peace . . . "

We owe to Isaiah the first association of the Messiah with the ideal of peace. I have a fondness for the passage in Isaiah 9:2–7 which dates back to 1915 when my sister and I sang in a Christmas cantata. I suspect it was her idea—she always hatched the wild ones. The reason I call this wild was that we couldn't sing, at least, not by any of the usual standards. We had never had any lessons. Not that we admitted that, then. We sang a great deal for our own pleasure, but Fort Smith did not clamor for us to sing publicly.

They let us sing in that cantata, though, and I have always been glad, for it was one of the most enriching experiences we ever had. The joint choirs of the town and a few strays, like us, met often and worked hard, and by the time the night came— Christmas Eve—she and I knew the whole cantata by heart, male parts and all! And for many years, whenever we were together in December, we would sing together some of the lovely arias and duets.

One of the songs for male voices was based on this chapter from Isaiah: "The people that walked in darkness have seen a great light: they that dwell in the land of the shadow of death, upon them hath the light shined. . . . For unto us a child is born, unto us a son is given: and the government shall be upon his shoulder: and his name shall be called Wonderful, Counselor, The mighty God, The everlasting Father, The Prince of Peace."

There's a sonorous roll to those words which seems to require music. There's a lift, both in the music I remember so well and in the meaning, as they mount to the climax!

Isaiah also used the word *Immanuel* (7:14), which means "God with us." Not—He *will be* with us, if we behave ourselves. There are no conditions attached, just "God with us" now, and always.

Listening to the news one evening, after the terrible typhoon and hurricane in Pakistan several years ago, I heard the announcer describe the awful condition of the survivors. He then gave the surprising information that Red China was sending as much aid in food and other supplies as all other countries, including the United States, put together! To make certain we had understood, he added, "Half of all received was from Peking."

Cynics might say that was only a political ploy, but I felt a lift of spirit. Maybe God has more faith in them than we have. Perhaps some Christmas the Red Chinese will say, "God with us."

Dave Garroway once wrote in *Faith Today:* "When you ask people what they want for Christmas, nine out of ten name something material. I used to be amused at it. Now I get irritated. Why? Because I happen to be one of those who can buy almost anything they want, and I've found they aren't so important after all. The one thing I'd really like for Christmas is *peace* in every sense of the word—peace of mind, peace of soul."

Here is some relevant advice from an anonymous author:

Ready for Christmas

"Ready for Christmas," she said with a sigh
As she gave a last touch to the gifts piled high.
Then wearily sat for a moment to read
Till soon, very soon, she was nodding her head.
Then quietly spoke a voice in her dream,
"Ready for Christmas, what do you mean?
Ready for Christmas when only last week
You wouldn't acknowledge your friend on the street?
Ready for Christmas while holding a grudge?
Perhaps you'd better let God be the judge."
She woke with a start and a cry of despair.
"There's so little time and I've still to prepare.
Oh, Father! Forgive me, I see what you mean!

To be ready means more than a house swept clean.
Yes, more than the giving of gifts, and a tree.
It's the heart swept clean that He wanted to see,
A heart that is free from bitterness and sin.
So be ready for Christmas—and ready for Him."

There is one more thing that goes into the Christmas Spirit: *goodwill*, which means *love*. This is the miracle-working ingredient, the one that opens our hearts to the world. Almost everyone remembers at this time that God so loved the *world* he gave his son; and hopefully they remember that "all people" are included in his beneficent grace.

If only this one element lasted! If we could be the faithful ones we sing about, what a change would take place:

> O come, all ye faithful,
> Joyful and triumphant,
> O come ye, O come ye to Bethlehem.*

Henry Van Dyke once said, "If you can keep Christmas for a day, why not always? *But you can never keep it alone!*"

Have you ever heard the story of Hilda, a middle-aged washwoman who lived in Detroit many years ago? When she parted her curtains one Christmas morning and looked out on a snowy world, she saw a thin little girl's face looking out a window of the shack across the alley. It looked hopefully first in one direction, then the other. All day, whenever Hilda looked out, she caught a glimpse of the little watching face. She began to fear the child was looking for Santa Claus. Finally, at nightfall, she could stand it no longer. She put her shawl on, took one of her few oranges, and went over. It was just as she feared. The mother had a night job, and the father was dead. The child was crying at a rickety table from which hung a little empty stocking.

* "O Come, All Ye Faithful," Translated from Latin, *Adeste Fideles*, by Frederick Oakeley.

Hilda lied valiantly: Santa was too busy to get around and do everything in one day. He would come yet. The child went hopefully to bed, and Hilda to a restless night. She had only one plan—to ask her family, the one she worked for, for help.

She started off early the day after Christmas, and got there before the father had gone to work. She told her story and the family rose to the occasion. The children brought toys; the mother got food and clothes. The father went with Hilda to the place where the child lived. He never forgot the bleak bare room, the pathetic little stocking, the child's transfigured face when they went in with their overflowing baskets. He was a cartoonist on a Detroit daily newspaper. Next December he drew a picture of that room and child. Below it he put one word: "Forgotten." He took it to the editor, who said, "We can't print that. It would spoil Christmas for a lot of people."

"Only for those who have thought of no one but themselves, and that's what I want to do."

"All right," said the editor. "We'll run it." So they did. After that it was run many times on Christmas morning and made its creator—Tom May of Detroit—famous. It was called, "The picture that opened a million hearts."

The Christmas Spirit is very real. It accomplishes a great deal. It puts a lot of goodwill into the world. Some of it is only temporary, true. But some of it bears lasting results.

Sometimes people who get absorbed and bogged down in purely selfish and personal concerns may, without realizing it, allow their complaints and bad temper to obscure the Christmas message for others—which reminds me of the littlest angel in the Sunday School Christmas pageant, who became either a comic character or a nuisance, depending on how you looked at it. She hadn't the least understanding of what she was taking part in and was always darting away on little excursions of her own. An older and more responsible angel would grab her, or chase her and coax her back. Once the cherub made a horrible face, and everyone knew a yell was imminent, but the older angel clapped a hand over her mouth just in time.

An additional funny touch was her halo, which was too large and kept falling down over her eyes. The audience didn't mind—they loved it. But the women putting on the pageant were provoked, because these antics were overshadowing the solemn message of the pageant. They didn't want any comedy to be included. So that little angel wasn't very popular backstage!

Sometimes grown-up people act very much like the littlest angel, and in them it is neither funny nor endearing. If the heart is warm and loving, physical conditions don't matter. If the heart is not involved, Christmas is an empty season.

> The door is on the latch tonight,
>   The hearth fire is aglow;
> I seem to hear soft passing feet—
>   The Christ Child in the snow.
>
> My heart is open wide tonight,
>   For stranger, kith, or kin;
> I would not bar a single door
>   Where love might enter in.
>   —Anonymous